Computers and Reading Instruction

Computers and Reading Instruction

LEO D. GEOFFRION

and

OLGA P. GEOFFRION

**ADDISON-WESLEY
PUBLISHING COMPANY**

Reading, Massachusetts
Menlo Park, California
London • Amsterdam
Don Mills, Ontario • Sydney

Intentional Educations, Series Developer
Peter Kelman, Series Editor
Richard Hannus, Cover Designer

Photo Credits: Chapters 1, 2, 4, 5, 6, 7, 8, David Shopper Photography; Chapter 3, Bruce M. Wellman; Chapter 9, Carol A. Trowbridge

Figure Credits: Figs. 3.1, 3.2, 3.3, and 3.4 are reproduced courtesy of VisiCorp.

Library of Congress Cataloging in Publication Data

Geoffrion, Leo D.
  Computers and reading instruction.

  (Addison-Wesley series on computers in education)
  Bibliography: p.
  Includes index.
  1. Reading—Data processing. 2. Computer-assisted instruction. I. Geoffrion, Olga P. II. Title.
III. Series.
LB1050.37.G46 1983   428.4′028′5   83-8727
ISBN 0-201-10566-7

ISBN 0-201-10566-7
ABCDEFGHIJ-AL-89876543

Foreword

The computer is a rich and complex tool that is increasingly within the financial means of schools. Like any educational tool, it comes with inherent advantages and disadvantages, is more appropriate for some uses than others, is more suited to some teaching styles than others, and is neither the answer to all our educational ills nor the end of all that is great and good in our educational system. Like any tool, it can be used well or poorly, be overemphasized or ignored, and it depends on the human qualities of the wielder for its effectiveness.

The purpose of The Addison-Wesley Series on *Computers in Education* is to persuade you, as educators, that the future of computers in education is in your hands. Your interest and involvement in educational computer applications will determine whether computers will be the textbook, the TV, or the chalkboard of education for the next generation.

For years, textbooks have dominated school curricula with little input from classroom teachers or local communities. Recently, television has become the most influential and ubiquitous educator in society yet has not been widely or particularly successfully used by teachers in schools. On the other hand, for over one hundred years the chalkboard has been the most individualized, interactive, and creatively used technology in schools.

Already, textbook-like computerized curricula are being churned out with little teacher or local community input. Already, computers are available for home use at prices comparable to a good color television set and with programs at the educational level of the soaps. If teachers are to gain control over computers in education and make them be their chalkboards, the time to act is now.

Each book in the *Computers in Education* series is intended to provide teachers, school administrators, and parents with information and ideas that will help them begin to meet the educational challenge computers present. Taken as a whole, the series has been designed to help the reader:

- Appreciate the potential and the limits of computers in education.
- Develop a functional understanding of the computer.
- Overcome apprehension about and fear of the computer.
- Participate in efforts to introduce and integrate computers into a school.
- Use the computer creatively and effectively in teaching and administration.
- Apply a discerning and critical attitude toward the myriad computer-related products offered in increasing volume to the education market.
- Consider seriously the ethical, political, and philosophical ramifications of computer use in education.

Practical Guide to Computers in Education is the basic primer for the series. *Computers and Reading Instruction* is one of a number of books in the second tier of the series, each dealing with computer applications in particular educational contexts. Other books include *Computers in Teaching Mathematics; Computers, Education, and Special Needs;* and *School Administrator's Guide to Computers in Education.* Still other titles are planned for this part of the series, including ones on computers and writing, business education, science, social studies, and the elementary school classroom. Each book in this second tier picks up where the *Practical Guide* leaves off. They are more focused and provide far more practical detail to educators seriously considering computer use in their schools and curricula.

Like the *Practical Guide, Computers and Reading Instruction* is a ground-breaking effort. It is the first available comprehensive presentation of the ways computers can be used effectively for teaching reading. Each chapter is filled with examples of useful computer applications and descriptions of actual computer programs, as well as ideas for future development by the classroom teacher and the industry. This is a pragmatic book, based on the authors' experiences, research, and thorough survey of promising practices in the field. At the same time, it is a forward-looking book which recognizes that current applications in reading fall short of tapping the vast potential of computers.

As series editor, I am confident that reading specialists and other teachers responsible for their students' reading instruction will find *Computers and Reading Instruction* to be a practical addition to their professional libraries, as well as providing food for thought and imagination.

Peter Kelman
Series Editor

Preface

What's all this talk about computers in my reading classroom?

Do I have to become a computer programmer to use them?

How can these machines help my students to improve their reading skills?

Questions like these are in the minds of educators throughout the nation as the computer revolution steadily moves into the classroom. Computers and their accessories are one of the fastest growing educational resources. After mathematics, reading and language arts instruction is the second most popular educational use for computers.

The remarkable versatility of computers is the major cause for their growing popularity in schools. Unlike most machines that are capable of only a few tasks, computers can be programmed to perform a multitude of tasks. Because programs are merely sets of instructions, they can be changed or modified instantly. At one moment the computer might calculate grades and at another tutor students or present learning games. No other single machine rivals this versatility.

Adapting this versatility to the reading needs of children is the biggest challenge facing developers of computer-based curricula. The ideal program teaches important reading skills in a way that takes full advantage of computer capabilities.

Effective computer-based reading instruction is the product of careful attention to both reading instruction and computer technology. A program in which students do little more than instruct a computer to display page after page of text reduces the computer to a very expensive page-turner.

Likewise, curriculum developers must keep in mind the underlying instructional objectives. Excessive use of graphics, lively animation, and sound effects basically turn some programs into video games. While children find the games exciting, it is unclear what reading benefits they gain from them.

The earliest attempts at computer-based reading and language arts instruction are, for the most part, imitations of traditional workbook activities. The simplest versions merely present text and match student responses against a template. Correct answers are reinforced by praise, graphics, or the awarding of points; and errors are immediately indicated to the student.

The use of computers as electronic workbooks turns them into surrogate or assistant teachers whose role is to dispense instruction and evaluate performance. At best, the teacher manages the computer by assigning computer lessons to individual students, but does not control the specific child-computer dialogue. In extreme cases, the electronic workbook becomes a "teacher-proof" curriculum that eliminates the teacher's capacity for involvement in the lesson. Several other potential educational roles for computers deserve consideration.

A Learning Tool

A tool enables a person to perform tasks that might otherwise be too cumbersome or awkward. The functionality of the tool is directly related to its helpfulness and convenience of use. For example, few people while reading bother to consult printed dictionaries because of the effort usually required; by the time readers get the dictionary, locate a word, and read its definition, they may well have forgotten the story line of the text. However, if text is presented by computer, it is possible to view definitions without looking away from the video screen. On-line dictionaries can make computers a more convenient medium for reading than conventional print.

An Educational Toy

Play is essential to child development and is a powerful vehicle for social and cognitive learning. Text-related play lacks the excitement and dynamism of other types of play; it is often difficult to create environments that allow children to manipulate text in interesting ways. Consider, for example, a traditional toy such as children's alphabet blocks. A child can arrange them into words, but the action produces nothing different from a random arrangement of the blocks. On the other hand, if the blocks were connected to a computer, it could say the word formed, draw a picture of the word, or create other activities involving that word. Toys like this could accelerate reading acquisition by providing young children with opportunities to play with text.

Microworlds

The ability to create highly motivating microworlds is a more radical intervention. Computers can create small worlds that students explore freely. For example, a student can rearrange reading topics to suit personal interests and needs. The student can even become one of the characters in a story and directly influence its outcome. In content-area reading, the student can select more detailed, or more cursory, explanations of text segments, depending on personal reading goals. At present, this type of environment is nearly impossible to attain through conventional means.

While the electronic workbook is currently the most pervasive form of educational software, we believe that the above alternatives merit greater attention. Individual chapters of this book describe a variety of reading approaches that are more consistent with current reading theory and exploit more fully the computer's versatility. Many programs described in the book are sold commercially while others do not yet exist, even though all are within the capability of modern small computers.

We have written this book with two major audiences in mind: teachers who wish to incorporate computers as effective tools in the reading classroom, and curriculum developers who want ideas for educationally relevant programs. We hope to accommodate the interests of both groups.

Chapter 1 opens with a summary of the bewilderment facing a teacher's first introduction to the world of computer-based reading instruction. Complex terminology and strongly held misconceptions often mask the computer's potential to revolutionize the teaching of reading.

Chapter 2 introduces computer terminology and the accessories used for reading instruction. It emphasizes the functional organization of the computer components and their value for reading teachers.

Chapters 3 through 8 examine the role of computers in various aspects of reading skill development. Each chapter demonstrates how psycholinguistic approaches to reading instruction can be adapted to computer-based instruction. We present many vignettes of children using computers and descriptions of actual and potential reading software to help clarify appropriate instructional roles. Some vignettes are based on real people and events, although the names and descriptions have been modified to protect privacy. Others describe fictional characters in hypothetical situations. Chapter 9 gives suggestions on evaluating reading software.

The Resources section contains a bibliography of publications and information about available reading programs, including public-domain software, major curricula, and individual programs to develop specific reading skills. In compiling the Resources section, we have tried to be as comprehensive and accurate as possible, although in a lively market such as computer-based education, it is nearly impossible to maintain complete records. New software emerge almost daily, often from small, obscure companies. Wherever possible, we have based the synopsis of each program on personal examination of the material. The inclusion of specific programs in the Resources section or in the main narrative does not constitute an endorsement of those products.

Several people have helped in the production of this book. We gratefully acknowledge the assistance and guidance of the series editor, Peter Kelman of Intentional Educations, who worked closely with us in the preparation of the manuscript. Nancy Via helped locate and examine programs for the Resources section. Additional ideas and suggested activities were provided by Art and Betty Bardige and Jeff Nilson. Carol Trowbridge, Peter Gordon, and Superscript Associates helped edit the manuscript and assemble the illustrations. We also thank Irene Athey, Ruth Lambert, R. Porter Cummins, and George Mason who reviewed drafts of the book.

February, 1983

Leo D. Geoffrion
Olga P. Geoffrion

Contents

Computers and
Reading Instruction

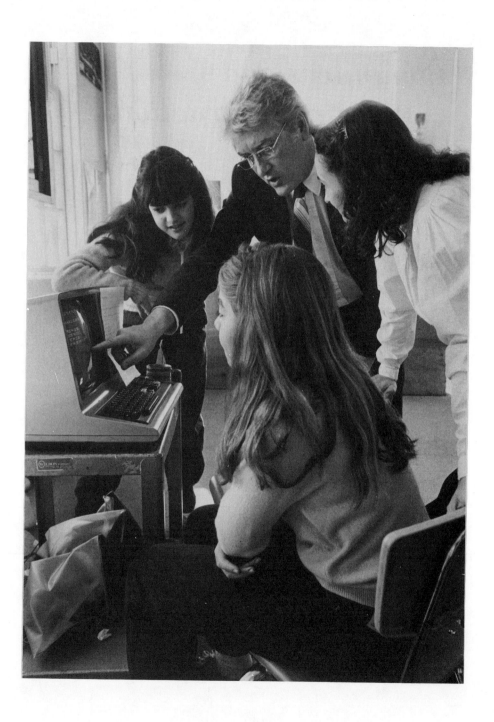

The Computer-Based Reading Classroom

1

Helen Sawchuck is a reading teacher at the Willistown Middle School. Her school, like many across the nation, has begun acquiring microcomputers for student use. She has observed from afar the computer, mounted on an audiovisual cart for easy transfer among classrooms and looking like a small, gray box with a typewriter-like keyboard and television-like monitor attached to it by cables.

Each week, the computer is brought to a different classroom. So far, mathematics teachers have monopolized it, using it to introduce computer literacy. Students learn the parts that make up a computer and are introduced to BASIC, a programming language that comes with the computer. They are occasionally allowed to play simple video games. A few students who show special talent and interest study programming more intensively.

The school principal has encouraged Helen to start using computers in her reading classes. Neighboring schools have reported dramatic gains in reading-achievement test scores as a result of computer-based programs. The principal has offered Helen a modest budget to acquire similar programs and test them in her reading classes.

Helen is willing to try computers but is not totally convinced of their value in reading instruction. She is also somewhat intimidated by them, having enough difficulty operating some of the audiovisual equipment already in the reading center. She is apprehensive about running a computer and wonders whether she will have to learn a programming language. After all, it has been years since she took a mathematics course. The few magazine articles she has read about computers are filled with strange jargon like "bytes," "buffers," and "disks."

Helen attends the state reading conference, hoping to gain insight into computer reading programs for her school. While computer exhibits were rare at a reading conference a few years earlier, this time several major publishers, and numerous small ones, are exhibiting computer-based reading programs.

One company offers a full computer-based reading curriculum, including diagnostic tests to determine student needs, drills keyed to individual skills, and a management system that provides detailed information on the progress of each student. The price of the curriculum is high, but the sales representative points out that it includes a computer specifically designed for this program and several student terminals. In the brochure photographs, children work diligently at individual terminals, and impressive-looking charts show their academic gains. Helen watches a demonstration of the program. Workbook-style questions appear on the screen, and the computer corrects student mistakes immediately.

A second company has adopted a different approach. It sells a series of short programs that are to be used with a small personal computer. The sales representative slides a square card called a "disk" into the machine, types in mysterious-looking commands, and the lesson begins on a television screen. This program also asks questions, but it reinforces correct answers with cute, animated pictures. A small shark-like monster, moving across the screen and eating up the correct responses, evokes smiles of amusement in the audience.

A third company emphasizes computerized reading games such as word-search puzzles, cryptograms, and "hangman" spelling games. The computer rapidly generates new challenges, scores the correctness of student responses, and praises high scorers. The games resemble those Helen's students have played for years using pencil and paper. Nevertheless, the computer versions seem more exciting. The sales representative points out that the content of each game correlates with the reading vocabulary in the basal readers of major publishers. There are options that allow Helen to add her own words to the activities. While the activities look interesting, she wonders if they are worth the price—particularly since they can easily be replicated using inexpensive ditto handouts.

A fourth company does not offer reading software, but advertises a programming language called PILOT, which is supposed to simplify writing computer-based lessons. The sales representative claims that, with this language, Helen can write her own lessons for the class. The sales demonstrations seem simple enough, and the computer displays look impressive, but the lessons generated look disturbingly like the workbook exercises that generally bore her students.

Helen also attends some conference presentations. In one, a university researcher describes an exciting array of futuristic devices, including machines that read aloud to students, show movies with strange special effects, and present text in unusual ways. Helen doubts whether any of these innovations are practical for her school and whether her school can afford them. She also wonders whether the teacher of the future will merely operate a room full of machines.

Helen's doubts are representative of those entertained by reading teachers throughout the nation. Computers are increasingly common in classrooms. While their role in mathematics is self-evident, their role in reading and language arts instruction is less obvious. After all, computers work with numbers, while reading involves letters.

Some of Helen Sawchuck's worries stem from the popular myths that surround computers and their operation. For many people, computers are sinister, invisible beasts. Whenever a problem arises in Helen's charge account, the store claims it's a computer error. News stories about unseen computer banks that hold vast amounts of personal information foster the image of the computer as Big Brother. Motion pictures and television frequently portray computers as dangerous monsters that destroy their creators or initiate global war.

With such strong negative impressions, people forget that computers are tools, no different in that respect from other machines. Computers are no more effective than the people who control them. An auto mechanic can use computer-based analyzers to tune an engine. The equipment makes the job easier and faster but cannot prevent the mechanic from incorrectly tuning the engine. Likewise, computers can facilitate education, but only if teachers become skilled in their appropriate use.

The thought of computer-based reading instruction evokes for Helen the image of a room with row after row of terminals. Before each terminal sits a child mesmerized by the computer displays. While the children become adept at computer-based skills, they lose the ability to interact with each other.

Following the advice of her principal, Helen visits Ray Hernandes's fourth-grade class in a nearby community. His class is organized into several learning stations, two of which have computers. During the day, children rotate through these stations. At the computer stations, children may work in pairs if they wish.

In the first period, Helen watches two boys, Tom and Brian, use a computer-based spelling game. The computer presents a scrambled word on the screen along with helpful clues. The boys get points for typing the word rapidly and correctly. They eagerly take turns guessing, each trying to outscore the other. Even when it is Brian's turn, Tom cannot resist volunteering additional clues and advice. They talk nonstop throughout the session.

In the next period a girl, Maria, plays a computer-based adventure game in which the computer presents a block of text, followed by a series of choices. When Maria selects one option, the computer displays the section of text that incorporates the consequences of her decision and poses a new challenge. Maria wins the game when she discovers a path to the buried treasure. Several times she calls on Monica, the class expert in this game, for advice on how to respond to certain episodes.

In the third period, two gifted students, Martin and Heather, are editing a classroom newspaper. They review the report on a recent field trip and discuss ways to make the story more appealing to readers. Heather decides that it needs a more personal focus and Martin wants to add an example. They go to the computer and enter some commands to display the current draft of the story. In a few minutes they revise the story, and the computer neatly reprints it with the desired changes in place.

During a break, Helen plies Ray Hernandes with questions. Her enthusiasm and her growing interest in computer-based instruction are evident. Ray confirms that most children prefer to use the computer with a friend even when the computer program is designed for individual participation. They transform it into a cooperative game by taking turns, or by working together to complete a task. The computer has inspired many new friendships, as conversations extend to other activities. Overall, Ray believes that the computer has stimulated social interaction among his fourth-graders. Indeed, his only complaint is that he occasionally needs to tone down the discussions, which have a tendency to be lively.

By the end of the day, Helen is intrigued by what she has witnessed among Ray's fourth-graders. She would like to bring some of this excitement to her own reading classes. Ray's comments suggested that she didn't have to be a computer scientist to operate computers. This dispels her lingering fear. Encouraged by the day's events, Helen resolves to embark on a new adventure with computer-based instruction.

WHY USE A COMPUTER TO TEACH READING?

Books, magazines, and other print media are fairly inexpensive, portable, durable, attractive, and efficient. A typical paperback book of 250 pages, selling for about five dollars, contains over 10,000 words and can provide readers with several days of enjoyment. A classroom can be supplied with a broad diversity of printed material at an annual cost of about $70 per student. Why introduce computers into the reading classroom when books serve reading so effectively?

Novelty

Novelty is the advantage most often associated with computers. Computers transform the dullest task into an adventure. Children who say they hate reading or mathematics practice these skills without complaint on a computer. While novelty may be a powerful force, its influence is ephemeral. As children and adults become accustomed to this new technology, their interest in computer-based reading activities will wane if these activities fail to address their reading needs and fail to exploit fully the computer's potential.

Dynamic Text

52

You ride with the gold shipment to San Francisco. On the first day of the trip, you have to go through a pass between two great rock walls. You round a bend only to find that the trail has been mostly washed out by a flash flood. It is getting late in the day. Scotty MacLeod, the driver of the coach, asks if you think he should try to get through even though you may get stuck.

While inspecting the trail, you find evidence of a recent campfire. It could mean bandits are in the area—and this would be an ideal place for a holdup.

If you tell Scotty he should try to get through as fast as possible, turn to page 80.

If you decide to wait and try to find out whether there are bandits nearby, turn to page 100.

Fig. 1.1 Dynamic text without computers.

Source: Edward Packard, Deadwood City *(New York: J.B. Lippincott, 1978), p. 52. Copyright © 1978 by Edward Packard. By permission of Harper & Row, Publishers, Inc.*

One characteristic of computers more likely to ensure their survival in the classroom is the capacity to change substantially the nature of print. Books are inherently static: the reader cannot rearrange the structure or contents of most printed material. Computers, on the other hand, are dynamic. They can be programmed to adjust their contents to the interests and needs of the user. A dynamic storybook format can encourage greater student participation in the plot development. While a few writers have attempted to create such stories in traditional print media, the result, as shown in Fig. 1.1, has usually been somewhat awkward.

The same story format is more simply executed on a computer. The computer program records the student's selection and displays the appropriate page of text automatically. In the western story shown in Fig. 1.1, the computer could store information about the hero's earnings, winnings at the gambling table, and supplies. This information shapes the options available in latter parts of the story.

Flexible Descriptions

In content-area readings, the concept of dynamic text can be adapted to provide a more flexible approach in the presentation of new information:

When we eat food, our bodies cannot use the nutrients immediately. Food must first be digested. Digestion starts in the mouth where the teeth grind the food into a soft pulp. This is aided by saliva which moistens the food and starts to break down the food cells into simpler nutrients. Meanwhile, the taste buds test that the food is good to eat. If the food is spoiled or otherwise unfit to eat, it will have a bad taste to most people. . . .

Ready: **Define saliva**

Saliva   Suh-lie-vuh

Saliva is the fluid given off by the salivary glands which are located inside the mouth, underneath the tongue. Saliva consists of a mixture of water and acids which help to break the food into simpler forms. Saliva serves to soften food before it is swallowed.

Ready: **Show salivary glands**

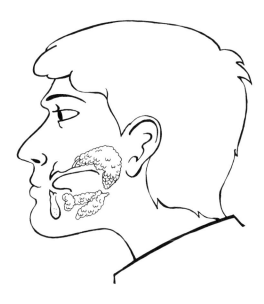

Ready: **Continue**

Here, the science text is transformed from a linear presentation of narrative to a matrix of information that a reader may explore freely. The reader may ask for descriptions of individual points, digress to related issues, or move quickly through uninteresting material. With books, students must flip pages and skim text to find a topic or area of interest.

Flexible text presentation is feasible because even small computers can store large quantities of information. A computer-controlled videodisk can store the equivalent of a 10,000-page encyclopedia on a disk the size of a phonograph record. Any individual page can be located and displayed in less than a second. With this storage capacity, more information can be included on such a disk than printed in most books.

Innovative Presentation Formats

Computer displays may lead to significant changes in how text is presented. Traditionally, books and other printed materials have had to present text in a compact format with small type to minimize physical bulk, even though it makes books harder to read. Consider the following excerpt from an automotive service manual:*

> If operation of the fuel pump is suspect, or it has been overhauled, it may be quickly dry-tested by holding a finger over the inlet pipe connector and operating the rocker arm through three complete strokes. When the finger is released, a suction noise should be heard. Next, hold a finger over the outlet nozzle and press the rocker arm fully. The pressure generated should hold for a minimum of fifteen seconds.

> **If** operation of the fuel pump is suspect,
> **or** it has been overhauled,
>
> it may be quickly dry-tested
>   by holding a finger
>   over the inlet pipe connector
>   **and** operating the rocker arm
>   through three complete strokes.
>
> **When** the finger is released,
>   a suction noise should be heard.
>
> **Next,** hold a finger
>   over the outlet nozzle
>   **and** press the rocker arm fully.
>
> The pressure generated should hold
>   for a minimum of fifteen seconds.

The text in these two versions is identical, yet the second version is easier to read because it is arranged by thought units, and key signal words are highlighted. If books were printed in this manner, they would have three times as many pages and be larger, heavier, and costlier. On the other hand, arranging a text by thought units requires only a 10 percent increase in computer space, because a computer stores text in compact form. When a computer displays text on a video screen, the additional number of pages does not increase cost as it would if it were printed on paper.

* Excerpted from J. H. Haynes and B. L. Chalmers-Hunt, *Toyota Corolla owners workshop manual* (Chatsworth, CA: Haynes Publications, 1975).

Integrated Presentation of Graphics and Text

Publishers of printed materials usually try to keep illustrations, diagrams, tables, and other non-prose material at a minimum because they add significantly to publication costs. Computers, however, store pictures in much the same way as text, and their inclusion adds little to the production costs of computer-based reading materials. Computers can also execute multicolored illustrations at a fraction of the cost in a book.

The capacity of computers to animate illustrations is particularly useful. Whereas a book must present the changes in an object through a sequence of static images, a computer displays every step of the object's evolution as a continuous process. The steps can be reversed, accelerated, or decelerated to emphasize the important changes.

On-Line Reading Tools

Reading tools such as a dictionary, glossary, thesaurus, and index are usually available to help readers comprehend difficult reading material. But many people prefer not to use them, because they intrude on the reading task. Looking up a word in a dictionary might require a few moments and interfere with the continuity of the material being read. When text is presented by computer, however, a person can instruct the computer to display a word's definition, and in seconds it appears in a corner of the screen without disrupting the main text. In similar fashion, a computer can show the previous appearances of any word in the text or provide a list of commonly used synonyms.

Speed

Computers can locate, record, and sort information quickly and perform calculations in millionths of a second. This enables a reader to find a piece of information far more rapidly than is possible in a manual search. The traditional printed index becomes obsolete when text is presented by computer. A computer can locate and display each page containing a particular word. Moreover, the reader can specify a search by multiple index terms. For example, the reader of a history text can instruct the computer to display all information on Supreme Court decisions before 1850. Multiple-search terms are not usually available in printed books.

Text Manipulation Tools

A word processor is a computer program that serves as a versatile writing aid with many powerful editing tools. A person can insert or delete words and sentences, rearrange paragraphs, or locate and replace misspelled words quickly and easily. Some sophisticated word processing programs can even detect common grammatical or stylistic problems.

When reading instruction is computer-based, teachers can use word-processing operations to build connections between the acts of reading and writing. For example, note taking is simpler when a reader uses the copy function of a word processor to extract key phrases from a text instead of retyping them manually. The reader can later rearrange these phrases into a coherent summary of the material read. Before reading one chapter of a book, a student could reread the notes for a synopsis of the previous chapters. Word-processing operations can permit a student to locate all mention of certain places or characters and keep track of a complex plot in a novel. Synopses and notes can also serve as the starting point for book reports and other writing projects. A student could also gather a file of favorite words to use in essays.

PEDAGOGICAL ASSUMPTIONS

Computers are the latest instructional innovation. Publishers are rushing new computer-based curricula into production, and even schools facing severe budget restrictions seem to find enough reserve capital to purchase computers for instructional use.

Computer-based reading programs must be founded on an understanding of both computers and reading instruction. Programs that ignore either element will be less than fully effective. A computer program with spectacular graphics and sophisticated computer operations is of little value if it fails to teach needed reading skills. Similarly, an electronic page-turner wastes the potential of a powerful instructional tool.

All reading instruction is ultimately based on teachers' beliefs and assumptions about the reading process and the optimal conditions for facilitating reading acquisition. It is our belief that reading is a psycho-linguistic process in which a reader uses a variety of skills to infer the writer's intended meaning. The cues that assist the reading process are phonic skills, linguistic skills, knowledge about the surrounding world, and problem-solving strategies. This view of reading leads to several assumptions about the optimal instructional approaches for teaching reading to students.

A Definition for Reading

Reading is the cognitive process of inferring meaning from the visual symbols commonly called print. Reading can assume many forms and serves a diversity of personal and social purposes.

- *Cognitive.* — Reading is more closely tied to thought and language than to motor or perceptual processes. Reading is learned by training the mind, not the eyes, or hands.

- *Inferred meaning.* — Comprehension comes from inside the mind, not from the text itself. Prior knowledge and experiences are valuable comprehension resources.

- *Visual symbols.* — Reading involves processes distinct from listening and speaking.

- *Print.* — Unlike pictographs, print consists of arbitrary codes that represent spoken sounds and meanings.

- *Many forms.* — People read a wide variety of materials, including books, newspapers, letters, instruction manuals, advertisements, and signs. Different materials usually call for different reading skills.

- *Diverse purposes.* — The purpose for reading shapes the skills involved. Reading for enjoyment is different from reading for information. Similarly, proofreading differs from skimming.

Effective instruction emphasizes the reading of prose over individual words and sentences. Reading involves multiple cues, including syntactic and meaning relationships as well as phonic patterns. When students learn to read primarily through word lists, they are denied the opportunity to use story structures to facilitate reading.

Comprehension should be the central focus of all reading instruction. Earlier reading theories saw comprehension as the outcome of several years of experience in learning reading skills. Recent theories show that comprehension is a central element to all phases of reading acquisition. Decoding skills cannot be fully applied without an understanding of the meaning relationships among the words in a text. Even the word "read" cannot be pronounced accurately without knowledge of its intended meaning:

Yesterday I read the first chapter and tomorrow I will read the next one.

Reading cannot be taught as a collection of isolated and specific skills. Mastery-learning models assert that complex academic skills can be reduced to a series of individual subskills, each of which should be taught until fully mastered. This premise fails for reading because the number and variety of its subskills remain unknown. Some taxonomies subdivide reading into as many as 2,500 subskills. If subskills exist, they are so highly interdependent that none can be taught in isolation.

Whenever feasible, child-centered instruction is preferred. People inevitably work harder and more carefully when they perceive a direct relationship between the work and their personal goals and interests. Reading instruction is more effective when it is tailored to the individual student's interests and preferred learning style. Schools seek to develop the social and psychological well-being of children; recognizing and accommodating individual student concerns and interests in reading instruction encourages this social development.

Foster active student involvement in the learning process. Children learn by interacting with their surroundings. These experiences become the raw material from which they develop and test their theories and models. In reading, children should be encouraged to reflect on ideas encountered, relate them to other experiences, and predict future outcomes. These activities are inherently more desirable than attempts to absorb material as isolated items distinct from other experiences.

The Computer 2

The early computer room was an inner sanctum, accessible only to an elite group known as *operators*, who performed mysterious rites amid a tangle of electronic boxes, blinking lights, whirling tapes, and printers that spewed paper at lightning speed. The operators spoke in an exclusive language intelligible only to their peers; and every switch and light bore a coded label. Computer rooms had separate power circuits, air conditioning, and special filters to eliminate dust and contaminants. This was clearly a world that mortals entered reverently.

Much of the aura surrounding the early computers has disappeared. Computers no longer require stringent environmental control, and there has been considerable progress in the development of machines that are easy to operate by novices. Thus, it would be appropriate for the computer and its operation to have a new and less intimidating image.

The mystery surrounding computers derives in part from the multitude of technical terms used to describe their components and operation. When stripped of this jargon, the technology is much less intimidating, and analogies to familiar organizations and activities become possible. (For a more thorough presentation, this chapter should be read in conjunction with Chapter 3, "Bits and Bytes" in the *Practical Guide to Computers in Education*, the first volume in this series.)

COMPUTER HARDWARE

The CPU

Think of a computer as a machine that operates like an office. The *CPU* or *central processing unit* is the office worker or clerk. It is the office manager of the computer and controls the operation of all the other parts. The CPU is a dedicated worker who never makes mistakes or becomes tired or bored. The CPU is also an unimaginative worker who always follows orders, without adding or deleting steps. This dutiful worker is, however, very fast and accurate—so fast that it can complete as many as 100,000 steps in one second!

The CPU itself comes in a variety of sizes. In *microcomputers*, it consists of a *chip* little more than one centimeter square. In large *mainframes* the CPU can be as large as a refrigerator. A mainframe computer is like a giant office with dozens of workers. The extra employees enable the large office to work faster and to complete many complex tasks simultaneously. Regardless of size, however, all CPUs perform the same tasks: receiving messages, carrying out operations, storing information in files, and communicating results.

Office workers cannot function productively without certain key resources. These include a desk where papers can be spread out while working, a file cabinet to store papers for later use, and some means of sharing information with others. In computer terminology, these are *memory*, *file storage*, and *input/output (I/O) devices*.

Memory

The computer's working memory is analogous to the clerk's desk. The CPU clerk works best when provided with a desk on which to spread out the current assignments. The larger the CPU clerk's desk, the larger the task it can complete at one time.

The desk has two major components: a standard office practices manual and a general work space. The standard practices manual tells the clerk how to perform the assigned task. This book is a permanent item, the contents of which can be modified only by upper-level management officials. The standard practices manual is seldom (if ever) modified.

The standard practices manual in computer terminology is known as *read-only memory* or *ROM*. The CPU can read instructions from ROM but cannot change its contents. The CPU always checks ROM and never deviates from its procedures. Only computer scientists, known as *systems developers*, can change its contents, typically by manufacturing a new ROM chip. The principal advantage of ROM is its permanence.

The remainder of the CPU clerk's desk consists of general work space, known in computer jargon as *random-access memory* or *RAM*. Random-access means that the computer can select any element of memory without disturbing the others. The CPU can read the contents of RAM and write information into it. RAM can be used to record messages, data, or instructions for later use, but its storage is only temporary and is erased at the start of each new computer program. Thus RAM is not suitable for long-term storage of information.

Since random-access memory is the principal work space of the computer, it is often used as an index of a computer's capacity. RAM size is measured in standardized units called *bytes*. In most computers, storing an individual letter or character requires one byte of memory space. Small computers typically contain between 32,768 and 65,536 bytes of RAM. This is described as "32K" or "64K" (1K equals 1,024 bytes).* A RAM of 48K is equivalent to about 20 single-spaced typed pages of information. In actual practice, however, that much text is seldom stored in RAM at one time, because that space is also needed for storing instructions and other material.

Storage Devices

A common office practice is to store information in file cabinets. For maximum efficiency, the contents of the file cabinets are neatly arranged into individual files that are properly labeled for easy retrieval. In computers, the file cabinets take many forms, but the most typical are devices that read and write onto a magnetic surface using a *disk drive*. Some small computers use a cassette tape recorder instead of a disk drive. While tape recorders are less expensive than disk drives, they are also slower and less reliable.

Disk drives have a storage mechanism that shares the characteristics of both RAM and ROM. As with RAM, the computer can both write onto the disk and read from it. Like ROM, contents of the disk are unaffected when the computer is turned off.

---

* One kilobyte equals 1,024 bytes, not 1,000, because modern computers are based on the binary number system. Two raised to the seventh power is 1,024, which is conveniently close to 1,000 for descriptive purposes.

Most computers have a large storage capacity. Microcomputers commonly use a five-inch *floppy disk* that can store about 150,000 bytes (150K), or the equivalent of 60 single-spaced typewritten pages. A floppy disk is easily removed from its drive without damage to the disk, thereby providing nearly unlimited storage capacity for those willing to change disks manually. Large mainframe computers frequently use one or more *hard disks.* Each hard disk can store up to 500 million bytes (500,000K) of information, but unlike the floppies, hard disks are not usually removed from the drives. Much of the floor space in large computer centers is devoted to hard disk storage.

Like office file cabinets, the contents of a disk are usually divided into files, each with a distinct identification label. The file cabinet analogy is not entirely accurate, however. In the case of office file cabinets, working

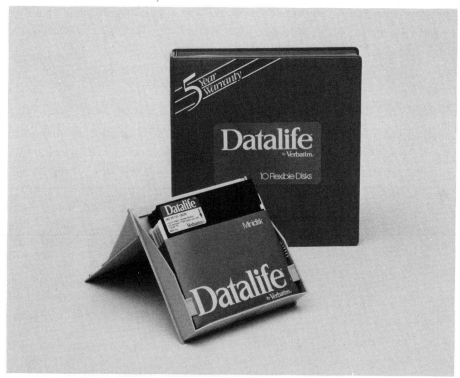

Floppy disks provide a convenient medium for storing computer files.
Source: Courtesy of Verbatim Corporation.

on a file requires physically removing that file from the cabinet. When a computer transfers a file into its working memory, it makes a copy of that file and leaves the original unchanged in the storage device. This safety feature allows the user to retrieve the file from the storage device when the contents of RAM are accidentally erased. This mode of information transfer adds versatility by simplifying the production of duplicate or backup copies as well as the development of edited versions of the file, without destroying the original.

Unfortunately, material recorded on disk by one computer can usually be read only by other computers of the same brand. For example, information saved on disk using an Apple II computer cannot be read by a TRS-80 computer. While the disks are physically identical, the information on them has been stored in a different recording format. Each computer also uses slightly different sets of instructions. Thus, different computers can only "talk" to each other through special communication *interfaces*.

Input/Output Devices

Finally, office workers need a way to communicate with people outside the office. Typically, office workers have several systems available to them: telephones, mail, courier services, and messengers. An efficiently run office reserves a separate space for each of these systems. In computer terminology, the communication equipment includes input and output (I/O) devices, while their work spaces are known as *I/O buffers*.

The most common input device is a *keyboard*. But the CPU can accept information from a variety of sources, such as telephones, special sensors, *game paddles*, and other devices. However, when an engineer designs a new input device, an interface must be built to ensure that the device deposits information in the input buffer in a format the computer can understand.

The most popular output device is a television screen or monitor (engineers call it a *cathode ray tube (CRT)*, or *video display terminal (VDT)*). Another common output device is a *printer*. Again, the CPU can send information to any machine that conforms to certain communication standards.

Computers can also communicate with each other by telephone. A special I/O device called a *modem* converts the computer's internal signals into tones that can be transmitted on telephone lines. When telephone messages are received, the same modem converts them back to computer signals.

COMPUTER SOFTWARE

Thus far, our office has workers, a desk, file cabinets, and communication systems. One crucial element is still missing, namely a system for accomplishing tasks. The CPU, disks, disk drives, and I/O devices are called *hardware*; the instructions they receive are called *software*. Software is a collective term for the commands that instruct the CPU in the effective use of the various hardware components. Software of different types can be thought of as commands for different kinds of activities taking place in an office. For example, the computer's *operating system* is like the standard procedures governing general office operations. A *computer program* can be thought of as the instructions for completing specific tasks. Various *applications* can be seen as client interactions.

Operating Systems

Operating systems, like standard internal office practices, establish the rules for file storage, the selection and operation of the various input and output devices, and the choice of *programming language* to be employed when communicating with users. The operating system provides a setting in which specific computer programs can be written as needed. *CP/M (Control Program for Microprocessors)* and *UNIX* are two common operating systems.

Because operating systems are usually highly complex, they are seldom modified by novice programmers. Indeed, their major function is to simplify computer usage by making available a wide range of computer operations without requiring that the programmer learn the details of the computer's internal structure. This is equivalent to an employee utilizing the services of a well-organized office without detailed knowledge of the office's internal procedures. Operating systems are usually modified by advanced computer scientists known as *systems programmers*. Systems programming requires more extensive knowledge of a computer's internal architecture than would be needed for most educational applications. In many microcomputers, the operating system is stored in read-only memory (ROM).

Computer Programs and Languages

Standard office practices can be applied to most office activities. But specific tasks often require a more detailed set of instructions. These instructions tell office workers how to use available resources to execute a particular job.

Computer programs are instructions that indicate the sequence of steps the CPU must follow to complete a specific task. The full set of available instructions is referred to as the programming language.

In the early years of computers, programming languages were limited command codes known as *machine language* and *assembly language.* Because these codes are in forms unlike human thought and conversation, many programmers find them difficult to learn and prefer to write programs using *high-level languages* more like English. High-level languages have special features that make them suitable for specific applications. Some languages used in schools are:

- *BASIC:* As a general-purpose language, BASIC is the most common language in small computers. BASIC is linear: the programmer usually writes commands in the order of their execution.
- *FORTRAN:* One of the earliest general-purpose computer languages, FORTRAN is usually available only in large computers and is less frequently used in education.
- *Pascal:* A newer general-purpose language, Pascal is widely used in computer-science programs. Pascal is modular, allowing the programmer to write complex programs as a series of simpler procedures.
- *Logo:* Logo is similar in structure to Pascal, but is easier to learn and more popular in educational programs. Logo has outstanding graphics capabilities.
- *PILOT:* PILOT is a special-purpose language designed for writing computer-based lessons. PILOT provides automated techniques for tabulating correct and incorrect answers, along with appropriate feedback.
- *COBOL:* COBOL is widely used in businesses and is particularly useful for inventory management, personnel record-keeping, and other commercial applications.

Programming in these high-level languages is usually taught in introductory and intermediate computer-science courses. While reading teachers can gain much from learning one or more programming language, such expertise is not essential in order to use most computer-based reading programs. However, teachers who know how to program can create their own computer applications and use their programming skills to customize programs written by others.

Applications

Interaction with the client, the third level of office activity, includes a client's request for a particular office service, the selection of options in that service, and the outside information needed to complete the task. A computer program needs the same information from the person using it.

A person who uses programs written by others is a *computer operator* or *user*. All the user needs to know is how to start and run a program. A program that has been well written is self-contained, user-friendly, and bombproof. A self-contained program does not require modification or user awareness of its internal complexity for effective operation. A user-friendly program is easy and convenient to operate. It uses interaction patterns that are natural and comfortable for adults and children alike. A bombproof program accommodates all possible user mistakes without disrupting program operation, making it impossible for naive users to damage or destroy the program or its operation.

Reading teachers who limit themselves to commercial software or to programs developed by others remain at the user level. Their principal concerns are in locating quality educational software. Chapter 9 provides suggestions for identifying good educational software.

THE COMPUTER AT WORK

Power-Up Sequence
on a Small Computer

Most small computers are designed for individual use. As such, they are turned on and off like common household appliances. When the user turns on the power, the following sequence of operations takes place automatically.

An Example of Self-Contained and User-Friendly Design

Modern computer printers often provide options that are activated through special print commands. In the first example below, the user must remember the complex syntax of the individual printer control messages. In the second example, the program asks a few simple questions and transforms the responses into the appropriate printer command. It finishes by confirming the new tab position selected.

A Poorly Designed Printer Program

ENTER SPECIAL PRINT FEATURES DESIRED:
PRINT CHR$(27);"A";CHR$(10);CHR$(27);CHR$(0)

A Well-Designed Printer Program

DO YOU WANT TO RESET THE HORIZONTAL TAB? **YES**
MOVE THE TAB TO COLUMN (0 - 80): **10**
THE HORIZONTAL TAB IS NOW SET TO COLUMN 10.

A Ten-Year-Old's View of How a Computer Runs a Program

Well, what happens . . . this is the mouth (pointing to the cassette recorder) and the computer eats the program off the tape. Then it goes through here (the cassette cable) like a straw, to the computer's stomach. Here's its face (the CRT screen) like a big eye, and you can look in and see what's in the stomach. . . . Then when you say RUN, the computer's got the energy to run 'cause it ate the program. If you don't load the program, it can't run 'cause there's no energy to. . . . You know what else computers eat? Potato chips. I hear there's lots of chips in these things.*

---

* M. M. Humphrey, All the scientists in the world smushed into one: What kids think about computers, *Creative Computing* Vol. 8, No. 4 (1982): 96–98.

On being jolted awake, the office worker opens the standard office practices manual (ROM) to the page containing instructions (operating system) on how to start the day (*boot-up* operations). These instructions typically include the following operations:

1. Clear the desk of all extraneous debris.
   (Clear RAM.)
2. Go to the file cabinet and get the handbook that indicates how the file cabinet's contents are arranged.
   (Transfer the *disk operating system* [*DOS*] into RAM.)
3. Place an "open for business" sign at the office door.
   (Output a "ready" message.)
4. Wait for a client request.
   (Wait for user input.)

Getting Started on a Large Computer

Large computers are designed to serve several users simultaneously, using a technique called *timesharing*. Instead of turning on the power, a *log-in* procedure is employed to identify each user. This typically includes the following steps:

1. The office workers are interrupted by a request for attention.
   (A user enters a log-in command at a terminal.)
2. The office requests the name of the person making the request.
   (The computer requests the user's name or identification number.)
3. The office verifies the person's identity.
   (The computer requests the user's password and compares it with the list of valid passwords.)
4. The office retrieves the person's file.
   (The computer retrieves the user's file from its disk. This includes information about files available and special command privileges accorded that particular user.)

Running a Program

To tell the computer to run a program previously saved, the user types the appropriate "run" command followed by the name of the file. This triggers the following sequence of operations:

1. Go to the standard practices book to find the correct procedures for "run".

    (Get from ROM the instructions on how to interpret the run command. These instructions might include steps 2–5 below.)
2. Go to the file cabinet and check whether the file exists and is the correct type for running.

    (Check the disk for file name and type.)
3. Clear the desk of all leftover information.

    (Clear RAM. This is done a second time in case something has been left in memory from a previous program.)
4. Move a copy of the file onto the desk.

    (Copy the file from disk into RAM.)
5. Do whatever the file indicates.

    (Execute the contents of RAM.)

Producing Text on Computers

The descriptions of computer hardware and software presented thus far apply to any setting. Computer-based reading instruction, however, poses special challenges for computer programmers.

Computers were originally designed for numerical analysis. Because early designers viewed print primarily as a way to label numerical results, many of the early computers were not designed to input, process, or display text efficiently. Although text manipulation, through word processing and filing systems, has been available since the first computers were introduced, only recently have computer companies devoted serious attention to the problems of text presentation.

Printers. Teletypes were the earliest output devices. These were heavy, noisy machines that could print only uppercase letters. Oddly, some modern computers continue this tradition and provide only uppercase letters. Moreover, the slow speed of teletypes prompted programmers to employ cryptic shorthand for computer messages.

Modern printers may be as small as a portable typewriter and produce both upper and lowercase print with excellent clarity. Some models even print in a variety of colors. The most sophisticated computer-controlled printers are actually phototypesetters, which produce text in a wide range of type fonts and sizes, using all the formatting options typically found in a professional print shop. However, because they are expensive to purchase and operate, phototypesetters are seldom used in educational programs.

The quality of computer-based printing is a joint result of the computer program that controls the printer and the mechanical quality of the printer itself. The program determines the physical page format and the content of the text, while the printer determines the size, style, and quality of the fonts available. Well-written programs give the user easy access to special printer features (see Fig. 2.1); less satisfactory programs may omit some features or may be awkward to use.

The quality of inexpensive printers is excellent but, at this time, of limited instructional flexibility. Typewriter-like printers do not permit a wide range of special effects, although they do provide options not possible on conventional typewriters. One such feature is the ability of some printers to produce characters twice the size of standard type. This makes much easier the production on computer of materials for beginning readers. Some developers of reading programs have tried to achieve extraordinary special effects using printers, such as the production of new vocabulary words in poster-sized print. While these make interesting murals, they are slow to produce and their value for teaching vocabulary is questionable. Few printers can produce pictures or other visual aids quickly enough for satisfactory interactive use with children.

Video.   Video-display terminals (VDTs), or monitors, are the most widely used computer output device. The principal advantage of VDTs is their capacity to produce a broad range of special effects. In addition to printing a word on a screen, a computer can be programmed to make the word flash, appear in color, change size, or move about on the screen. The speed of these effects can be controlled to fit instructional goals.

The least expensive VDT is a television set connected to the computer, although the video quality of standard televisions is usually inadequate for reading instruction. Letters displayed on a television screen are less distinct than on other VDTs and may vibrate slightly because of instability in the video signal. Some VDTs use green phosphor screens. These are often preferred to white phosphor because they are less tiring to read.

Illustrated Text_Editor

Have you ever wanted to use a picture instead of those one thousand words? Now there is a word processor system that lets you include your pictures along with the text of your message. The program is called DECRITE and it performs on your GIGI terminal from a VAX or a RSTS or a TOPS20 host computer. This ECS developed software is ideal for turning your ideas and class handouts into finished documents in the shortest possible time. Because the document generation, editing and final printing takes place with the same equipment you can exercise your creativity, proofread, and produce in a single sitting.

With DECRITE you can see typefaces as you select them and while they may not be as smooth as type from a typesetter, you do not have to wait for nor pay for the high priced spread. In fact, DECRITE and GIGI offer such a variety of typefaces that there are over 7000 printable character typefaces! They include boldface, *italics*, underline, and more. AND there are all the combinations of these!

Add color and blink to the list if you use DECRITE to develop electronic mail to be sent to GIGI users.

You can even edit directly in nearly any language using an appropriate character font. And within a given language, other styles can be used for special purposes, such as the "CREATE FORMAT" PREFERRED FOR OVERHEAD PROJECTIONS. In fact, you can mix languages within the same text, and since DECRITE references font files created ... the Character Set Editor, there is virtually no limit on how many different fonts may be used in the same document.

Customary usage sets off certain information such as titles in italics or underline. Now you will be challenged to discover new ways you can keep the reader's attention. ... use inverted video to convey sarcasm? Left italics could show your ... on an issue.

During your editing you can change margins and tabs as many times as you like too, thereby leaving "rulers" in the text. These margin and tab rulers along with picture "tokens" and character attributes can be cut and pasted elsewhere in your document. Have you ever hyphenated a word in your rough draft, only to have a gratuitous dash appear in the final copy? If you use the MENU key plus "-" for 'join' and "H" for 'hyphen', DECRITE places an invisible hyphen in the word to be used only if necessary. Or you can simply hit control/W to place an invisible hyphen. Naturally, the dash provides DECRITE with the option of doing word-wrap at that point. Have you forgotten where a hyphen or ruler or picture token or margin change was placed? Simply hit MENU and "OT" for 'Observe Tokens' and DECRITE will show you where these things are without distorting the character spacing or page layout!

DECRITE can also output any character that can be used as a DRAWN "dropped initial" as done at the beginning of this article. Headlines of these characters can be placed even across 14.5 inch width paper on the LA34VA printer.

Aside from the Relative Picture Files (RPF) that DECRITE produces for drawn letters, only the Graphics Editor (GE) can generate relative addressing ReGIS code which DECRITE requires for illustrations. This is done by using the GE command "extract (file name)". Picture files from Data Plotting Package (DPP) and ReGIS Application Library (RAL) must be converted this way for use by DECRITE.

You interact with text and do not have to "program" your layout. You have up to 20 tabs settable to over 700 pixel positions. And you can get automatic multicolumn text, automatic word-wrap, and automatic page headers and page numbering.

Relative Productivity of Software

[source: Tektronix]

Elapsed Time

Richard M. Merrill
Education Computer Systems

Fig. 2.1   Examples of special effects possible.

Source: Edu (Summer 1982): 5. Copyright, Digital Equipment Corporation, 1982. All rights reserved.

VDTs are not without problems, however. Many small computers have very limited text-presentation capabilities, which may be exacerbated by VDTs. For example, some microcomputers display only uppercase letters arranged on a 40-column by 24-line screen. The lack of lowercase makes the screen more difficult to read and makes computer-based reading lessons appear unlike print normally encountered by students. The 40 columns severely limit the amount of text that can be displayed at one time. New terminal designs, currently sold for office word processing, display 66 lines of 80-column print, the equivalent of a full printed page.

Print legibility is another problem. Terminals that display both uppercase and lowercase letters on a full 80-column-wide screen have, as a result, very small print that may be hard to read. Print legibility for such computer systems is particularly troublesome when a television or inexpensive monitor is the display device. Terminals purchased for use in reading instruction should be easy to read.

The possible health hazard resulting from long-term VDT use is of broader concern. While people usually watch television from a distance, a computer user sits only a few inches from the VDT and is subjected to greater eyestrain and larger doses of electromagnetic radiation. The long-term effects of such exposure are unknown, but some terminal users complain of headaches and visual discomfort. The results of studies by the National Institute of Occupational Safety and Health (NIOSH) suggest that eyestrain from video displays may be more problematic than any radiation hazard.

Interactive Video Devices.   One of the most exciting innovations in computer output, interactive video is a computer-controlled video-cassette or videodisk player. A video player can display large numbers of high-quality pictures and animations on the VDT. The computer can select among the video segments, stop at any point, superimpose text over the pictures, and replay segments in slow motion, accelerated motion, or even in reverse. All the lively detail of television thus combines with the computer's interactive capability. The *DAVID* system at the National Technical Institute for the Deaf in Rochester, New York is one of the better examples of interactive video applied to education.

To use interactive video, educators must have both a computer and a video-cassette or videodisk player equipped with remote control. A special

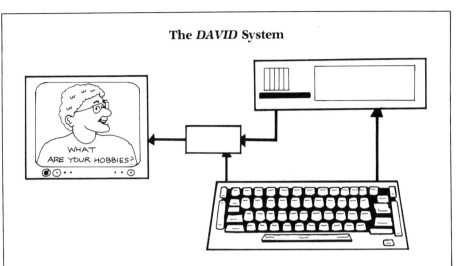

The *DAVID* System

DAVID was developed to improve the language skills of hearing-impaired college students attending the National Technical Institute for the Deaf. A special terminal receives video signals from both a video-cassette player and a computer. The computer controls the video player and superimposes questions on the television picture.

One *DAVID* lesson is a simulated employment interview used to teach communication skills. The video segments are filmed as though seen through the eyes of the person interviewed. It begins with entering the office of the personnel manager who, after greeting the viewer, asks questions about the viewer's interests. The video-cassette shifts to a different segment based on the viewer's answer to each question. The resulting interview is remarkably true to life.

interface circuit enables the computer to transmit signals through the remote-control connector on the video player, while a mixer combines the video output from the computer and player. The total cost of such a system, including the computer and player, is currently about $5,000. Video-cassette systems are better suited for experimental programs because cassettes can be erased and rerecorded easily when program modifications are desired. Videodisks are faster, more reliable, and yield a sharper picture than cassettes, but at this time disks cannot be erased, duplicated, or modified.

Educators have not as yet made much use of interactive video, partly because the technology is expensive, and partly because nearly all video-cassettes and videodisks currently sold are recordings of popular films not intended for educational use. Nevertheless, it is likely that the greater versatility of interactive video over conventional computer displays will lead to increased usage in the future. *The First National Kidisc*, distributed by MCA is an intriguing early example of the interactive capacity of videodisk. The disk contains a game to identify state flags, origami lessons, visual-perception drills, thrilling movie footage from the cockpit of an airplane, and other activities.

Computer-Based Speech Production.   Beginning reading is closely linked to a child's oral language. Nearly all modern methods for teaching reading develop strong associations between print and a child's speaking vocabulary. Thus, if a computer could talk as well as display text, it would be a very effective teaching tool for those who are not yet proficient readers. However, speech output remains a difficult computer task. None of the computerized speech production available now is adequate for reading instruction, and further development is necessary.

Synchronized tapes or records were the earliest approach to computerized speech production. Signals from the computer control the tape or record player, allowing the computer to select among messages prepared in advance and play them as needed. This is a more sophisticated cousin of the sound-filmstrip projectors used in schools, and a precursor to interactive video systems. Unfortunately, such synchronized speech devices have not proved reliable. The tape or record often drifts out of synchrony and plays incorrect messages. Some systems have overcome the synchronization problem by using stereophonic cassette players. One channel plays the audio messages while the other channel contains timing signals for the computer. Thus, the computer program can accurately control the tape position to avoid errors.

Digitally coded human speech is another approach to computer audio output. The computer controls a special interface called an *analog-to-digital converter* that transforms the speaker's voice into a string of numbers and stores them in computer memory. When needed, another electronic circuit known as a *digital-to-analog converter* reconstructs the original

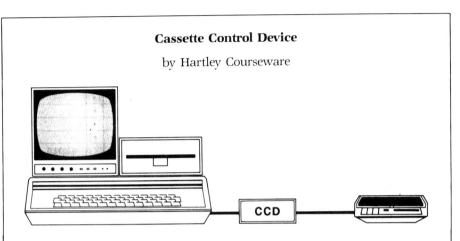

Cassette Control Device

by Hartley Courseware

The *cassette control device* (CCD) developed by Hartley Courseware is an example of an inexpensive synchronized speech device. The CCD is a relay switch that connects a computer to the remote control of a cassette player. The computer uses the CCD to start and stop the cassette player at predetermined intervals.

Audio stimuli, such as a list of words, can be recorded on the tape using a standard time segment for each word. The computer plays each word in sequence as required in the lesson. The audio quality is excellent and is only limited by the fidelity of the tape recorder. However, all speech must be recorded in sequence, and no word can exceed the time limit allotted to it. If the user is not careful to set the tape at the correct starting location, the wrong audio messages are played. Otherwise, the CCD produces accurate speech for phonics and reading lessons.

signal from these numbers and plays it through conventional audio amplifiers and speakers. Because this approach avoids the mechanical interface to a phonograph or cassette tape, it is more reliable than synchronized speech devices. However, the messages that might be required must still be digitized in advance. Furthermore, to produce realistic speech quality, considerable amounts of memory must be allocated to the numerically coded speech. In general, most small computers lack adequate memory to store both a moderately complicated instructional program and a variety of high-quality spoken messages. This type of audio is usually reserved for brief special messages.

Supertalker II: **A Digitized Speech Device**

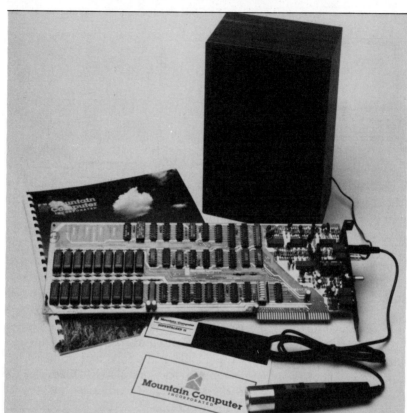

Reprinted with permission of Mountain Computer, Inc.

Supertalker by Mountain Computer is a typical example of a digitized speech device. Designed for the Apple II computer, it comprises an accessory circuit board, speaker, microphone, and software. When recording messages, the circuit card transforms the electrical signals from the microphone into a numerical code that can be stored in the computer's memory. Playing back messages reverses the process; the circuit card transforms the numbers into electrical signals for the speaker.

    Supertalker can be set to record and play at different memory speeds. The fastest, 4,000 bytes per second, produces high-quality speech, but only about 12 seconds can be recorded at this speed before the Apple II's 48K of memory is filled. Slower speeds, such as 500 bytes per second, permit longer messages but reduce intelligibility. Software that employ *Supertalker* usually store the messages on disk and load them into the computer as needed. This avoids consuming too much computer memory but also slows down the program substantially.

True synthetic speech is a third approach to audio output. No human speech is involved; the computer creates spoken messages as needed using a process similar to that of music synthesizers. Because each word is synthesized from its phonemes, an unlimited vocabulary is possible, and the special instructions necessary to produce the speech consume only a small portion of the computer's memory. Synthetic speech is currently the most versatile approach to speech production by computer. However, the voice quality of most devices available today is mediocre. It has a distinctly mechanical sound with limited control of inflection and tone, a significant defect if the synthesizer is to be used for developing reading fluency or phonic skills. However, with speech quality improving constantly, these devices should prove a useful asset to computer-based reading programs.

Entering Text on Computers

Keyboards. A keyboard is the most widely used method for entering text in a computer. It comes as standard equipment on virtually all computers, and, because of its similarity to the traditional typewriter keyboard, it is universally accepted.

While a computer's keyboard looks like a typewriter, it has several additional keys. Some control the position of the *cursor*, the point at which any text editing takes place. In computers with video display, the cursor is usually a small rectangle of light, while in printer-style terminals, it is the current position of the print head. Some keyboards have special keys for commonly used commands. For example, the "insert" key on the keyboard shown in Fig. 2.2 is used to add characters at the cursor position. The insertion displaces further to the right all text located to the right of the cursor position. These keys simplify typing by providing handy editing options. Some keyboards also contain a row of function keys, whose role can be determined by the computer program. These function keys are seldom used in most programs because they are not uniformly available on all keyboards. When used, they can further simplify the selection of

Personal Speech System: A Synthetic Speech Device

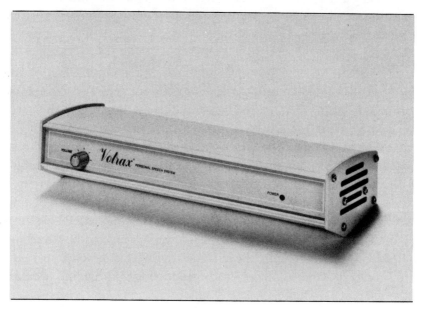

Source: *Courtesy of Votrax, a division of Federal Screw Works Inc., 500 Stephenson Hwy., Troy, MI 48084.*

The *Personal Speech System* by Votrax is an example of an inexpensive speech synthesizer. Physically, it consists of a small box that connects to any computer. The box contains a special-purpose computer that phonetically analyzes text, a speaker, and an amplifier. Because the human voice is not involved, a microphone is not needed.

A computer program produces speech by transmitting text to the synthesizer's special-purpose computer which, in turn, translates the text into the appropriate phonemes. These phonemes are then individually joined and transmitted to the audio speaker. Because the synthesizer builds each word, it has an unlimited vocabulary, but the print-to-speech computer occasionally mispronounces words.

program options or entering of complex commands. For example, in one word processor, a person can store words or sentences in buffers, each represented by a different function key. Pressing the function key prints the contents of its buffer automatically, simplifying the production of business correspondence.

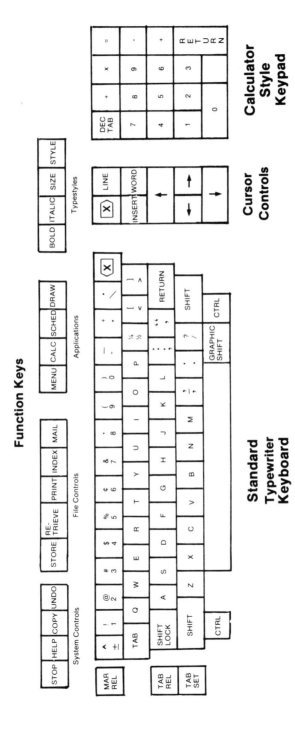

Fig. 2.2   Diagram of a full-function keyboard.

The Timex Sinclair 1000 Personal Computer with TS 2040 Thermal Printer and touch-panel keyboard.

Source: Reprinted with permission of the Timex Computer Company.

On a few microcomputers, the traditional keyboard has been replaced by a *touch-panel* or *membrane* keyboard. This is a smooth, touch-sensitive surface with the position of each letter laminated on the plastic surface. The membrane keyboard is less expensive to manufacture and better protected against damage from dirt and water than a traditional keyboard, but many people used to typing on keys dislike the way it feels.

While a keyboard may be convenient for experienced typists, it is often not the best input device for children. Unless a child already knows how to spell words and can type at a comfortable rate, a keyboard can be a burdensome nuisance. Most novice typists remember the confusion of looking for one letter among fifty closely spaced keys, all of similar shape and color. The nonalphabetic arrangement of keyboard letters is particularly problematic for beginners. Many multiple-choice educational drills require the student to select among four options, designated by the letters "A" through "D". While this is handy on paper, these letters do not have a simple and convenient keyboard arrangement. Thus, beginners must waste time searching for the correct key.

On the other hand, computer keyboards are more versatile than type-writer keyboards because most computers allow the programmer to assign a function to individual keys other than that indicated on the key face. In an activity calling for a true/false response, the left half of the keyboard might be designated as "true" while the right half becomes "false". This assignment of keys is particularly easy to do on a touch-panel keyboard. Plastic overlays can be attached to the smooth keyboard surface to indicate the new arrangement (see Fig. 2.3).

Computers can also be programmed to lock out or ignore certain keys. For example, if the selections in a multiple-choice task range from "A" to "D", the computer can ignore irrelevant keystrokes or remind the student that only "A" through "D" are acceptable responses. Locking out irrelevant keys makes a program simpler for novices.

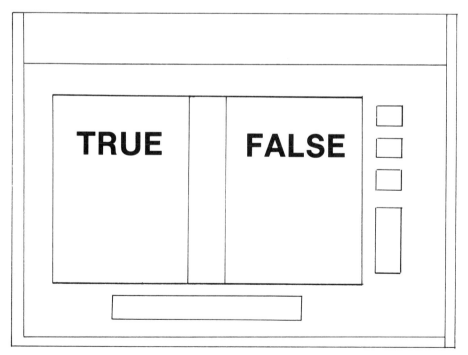

Fig. 2.3　Membrane keyboard with true/false overlay.

Game Paddle, Joystick, and Mouse. In addition to typing, a person can enter information in a computer using a variety of special controls connected to the *I/O ports* of the computer. Game paddles use a control knob that moves the cursor across the screen along any axis. Joysticks are fashioned after the control stick of early aircraft and move the cursor in any direction. A mouse is a small object that a person slides along any smooth surface. The computer senses the motion of the mouse and moves the cursor correspondingly. All three devices contain one or more switches.

Although these accessories are usually associated with arcade games, they are convenient response devices for educational activities as well. In a multiple-choice task, students could rotate a game-paddle knob to move the cursor to a selection and then press the paddle button to choose the item. This form of response is faster and easier for children who are not skilled typists.

Micromouse

Source: Reprinted courtesy of 3G Company.

Touch-Sensitive Screens and Light Pens. Some computers use a touch-sensitive screen that allows a person to make selections by touching a portion of the video screen. In a similar way, the computer can sense the location of a small light pen when it touches the screen. These devices permit a more natural interaction for novices. Students make selections by interacting with the screen instead of dividing their attention between the screen and the keyboard. For example, in a multiple-choice test, the student touches the correct answer on the screen itself instead of searching for the correct key on the keyboard.

Most touch-sensitive screens and light pens have been designed for engineering applications, and although they are useful, may not be ideal for very young children. Some touch-sensitive screens do not recognize a young child's small fingers or may produce errors if other fingers, in addition to the intended pointing finger, touch the screen. Light pens work best when carefully held perpendicular to the screen. Young children can be taught to use the light pens, but errors and missed inputs are frequent. Further development is needed before these can be fully effective in the classroom.

Voice-Entry Systems. The ideal device for entering text might be a computer that can recognize spoken commands. With such a device, children could answer questions orally or dictate experience stories to the computer. The computer could monitor the accuracy of a child's pronunciation during oral reading exercises.

The current voice-entry systems are only partly successful. Existing devices can recognize a small set of spoken words (usually less than 64). Moreover, the computer program must be taught to recognize each person's speech patterns. Considering the commercial desirability of a business machine capable of accepting dictation, more sophisticated voice-entry systems are likely to emerge in the near future.

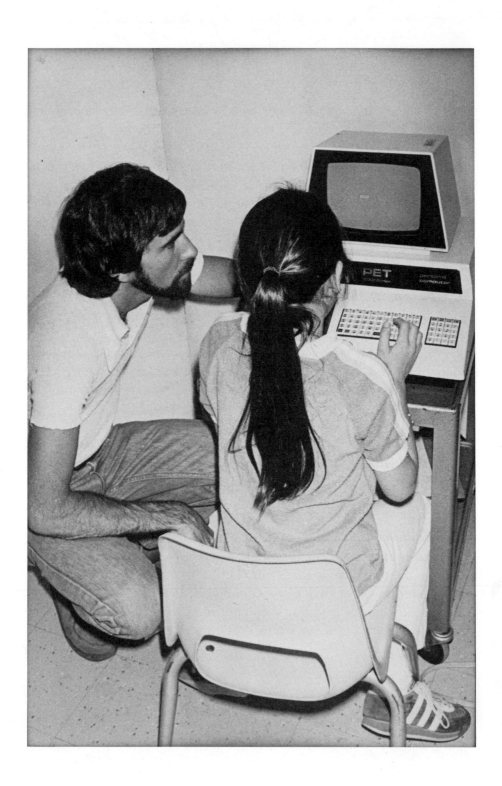

Reading Readiness   **3**

The prerequisite skills for reading acquisition remain unknown in spite of nearly a century of reading research and several centuries of teaching reading. Over the years, a broad range of prerequisites has been proposed and rejected. Among these are the beliefs that children must have attained a mental age of 6.5 years, have strong perceptual-motor skills, show good understanding of left-right orientation, or have achieved the cognitive stage of concrete operations. While all these factors are in some way related to reading, they are neither necessary nor sufficient for reading readiness. They are not necessary because individuals can be found who are good readers yet show poor development in these prerequisite skills. They are not sufficient because remediation of those skills does not automatically lead to improved reading readiness.

Part of the problem stems from perceiving readiness as a discrete developmental state clearly separate from reading. In some reading curricula, readiness instruction consists of exercises in the perceptual and motor skills that are presumed to underlie reading. Children may spend hours developing balance, eye-hand coordination, and left-right awareness because the teacher hopes these skills will lead to improved reading readiness. Studies of program effectiveness, however, consistently demonstrate that training in these skills neither improves reading readiness nor helps to remediate reading disabilities.*

Readiness is better seen as the initial stage of learning to read. As such, readiness instruction may be indistinguishable from reading instruction.

---

* For a review of the deficiencies in perceptual-motor training programs, see D. Hammill, "Training visual perceptual processes," *Journal of Learning Disabilities*, Vol. 5, No. 10 (1972): 39–46.

Wherever possible, readiness activities should be directly tied to introducing print and to developing a child's vocabulary, language, and cognitive skills. Four aspects of reading readiness are:

- Developing an awareness of print.
- Learning to identify the letters of the alphabet.
- Developing an initial reading vocabulary.
- Increasing language comprehension skills.

CHARACTERISTICS OF COMPUTER PROGRAMS FOR PRESCHOOLERS

At present, few computer programs address readiness instruction well, primarily because designing adequate input and output means for preliterate children is difficult. Printed instructions and responses are clearly inappropriate because readiness-level children cannot be expected to read or type accurately. This means a readiness program requires special devices not usually found on standard computer models, such as speech synthesizers, interactive video, and accessory switches.

Output Techniques

Because young children often have short attention spans, computer outputs must be highly stimulating. Video display is almost essential, with animation and speech production as valuable accessories. Animated, complex pictures are not necessary, but ample motion and sound help to sustain a child's interest.

Good animation and clear speech production are difficult to attain on many computers. Compared with television, microcomputers can present only simple pictures and actions. Large computers are more powerful, but the graphics terminals used with these machines are too expensive for most elementary school systems. Interactive video may be the most promising output device for young children because of its superior color, animation, and sound. The video player can present all the action and special effects possible in modern films and television, while the computer makes these interactive for the young child. Interactive video is also similar to television and therefore familiar to young children reared on "Sesame Street." Many of the activities described in this chapter lend themselves to interactive video, although currently such programs are not sold commercially.

Input Techniques

Input poses similar problems in reading readiness programs. Preschoolers enjoy pushing buttons, particularly when these produce dramatic visual effects, but they are very inaccurate when required to locate a specific key. Indeed, immature children often start by pounding the keys with the palms of their hands, elbows, or fists. This style of response is hard on the keyboard and on the computer program. At this stage of development, children show minimal awareness of the causal relationship between pounding the keyboard and any changes in the visual display. They recognize a global relationship between the two—if the display is turned off, they soon stop. They are unaware that they can control the display by pressing buttons selectively. As a result, their selections are generally random.

Later, children begin to press individual keys in a more deliberate manner. Simultaneously, they develop an awareness of the various keys and are eager to discover their individual functions. Typing remains a difficult task because most children this age do not know the alphabet, nor are they prepared for the visual and cognitive overload of locating the desired letter among 50 similar keys. A beginner may take three minutes to type one word correctly without adult help. Preschoolers clearly need alternatives to typing.

An expanded or simplified keyboard can ease the typing problem, but it also increases the price of a computer system. Touch-panel keyboards are the easiest to modify for readiness instruction. Because the keyboard has a smooth surface, overlays can be used to reduce the number of keys, rearrange their sequence, or add new labels to each key. In an introductory reading activity, the keys might be labeled with vocabulary words or pictures instead of individual letters.

Special switches for computer input are also possible. Most micro-computers can accommodate accessory switches. The switches can take any physical form, such as objects to push, rotate, tip, insert, or merely touch. A vocabulary development activity might provide a series of cards

Fig. 3.1　Computer with a slot machine.

with a word printed on each one. When a child inserts a card in a special slot machine (see Fig. 3.1), attached by cable to the computer, the word might be spelled in large letters on the video screen, followed by a cartoon depicting the meaning of the word, which then fades into the printed version of the word. In this manner, children could experiment with words before being able to spell them.

Presently, few commercial reading readiness software use special switches for young children. Most software developers have totally ignored the benefits these switches could offer preliterate children. This is partly due to the inadequate variety of ready-made switches. While game paddles and joysticks are available, most are too small and fragile for use by preschool-aged children. Fortunately, child-appropriate switches can be fabricated easily in a basement workshop for only a few dollars for parts.

When only a few responses are needed from the child, they can be displayed in a list. The program slowly moves a pointer through the list. This scanning procedure is used in Britannica's *Computer Animated Reading Instruction System (CARIS)* to help children select words. For example, in the following noun list, children select an item by pressing any key when the pointer reaches the word they want:

```
        HOUSE     BOY
        BOAT      CAR
   ⇒ TREE        TRUCK
        DOG       CAT
```

The scanning rate must be slower than two seconds per word to give children adequate time to examine a word and respond. This sharply limits the number of items possible. When more than about ten options are offered, scanning becomes too slow and confusing for young children.

With scanning systems, children must learn the pointer's function. Very young children often choose items in a seemingly deliberate manner but may be unable to select particular items on request. This is especially prevalent when all the items yield an interesting result. When prompted by an adult to look for a word, children sometimes respond by pressing a key as soon as they have visually located a desired word, even if the pointer is not at the target word.

User Control

Besides special switches, student control is another important design consideration in developing activities for very young children. The traditional drill-and-practice structure often used with older children is less effective with preschoolers because they are much less interested in answering questions posed by others. On the other hand, the same children may devote more time and effort to self-directed play. This difference in attention span is greatest in very young or immature children. Effective computer programs for these children minimize questioning and seek instead to develop environments that closely resemble play. In these, children are free to explore aspects of the program. The introduction of reading skills is less the result of direct instruction than a by-product of a child's efforts to manipulate the computer.

PRINT AWARENESS

The child's environment is full of printed messages: books, newspapers, signs, and advertising. Many children start to read these messages at a very early age. Even two-year-olds often recognize common signs and labels, usually by remembering the words from the surrounding context. These early experiences have a lasting effect. Dolores Durkin has shown that children who learn to read at an early age through informal experiences continue to be superior readers throughout their elementary school years. They also exhibit a strongly positive attitude toward reading. Early print experiences provide a foundation for later reading instruction by helping to make a child aware of print and its communication role.

The Components of Print Awareness

1. Knowledge of the organization of books.
   a. A story starts at the front of the book.
   b. Books are held in an upright position for reading.
   c. A book tells a consistent story which has a beginning, middle, and end.
   d. A story ends at the last page.
2. Awareness of text.
   a. Text, not pictures, tell the story.
   b. Text consists of words and letters.
   c. Punctuation marks add emphasis to the text.
   d. Reading a text involves left-right and top-bottom motion.
3. Respect for books.
   a. Books are not meant to be torn, thrown about, or otherwise damaged or destroyed.

Print awareness is best taught by providing children with many books and other printed materials relevant to their interests. However, exposure alone is insufficient unless a child is personally involved with the material. Story time is a prime example: an adult takes time to read to a child, and in turn, the child is drawn into the story through personal interaction with the adult. Children often enjoy having a favorite story reread many times. They remember details from it and may even be able to repeat the story from memory. When they can see the book as it is read, they begin to identify key words in it. Computerizing story time would be counterproductive because the personal involvement is a critical factor in its effectiveness. However, other types of computer activities can help to develop a child's awareness of print.

The *Talking Page*

The *Talking Page*, developed as part of the PLATO Early Reading Curriculum (PERC) Project by John Riskin and Priscilla Obertino, uses a creative approach to print awareness. The *Talking Page* displays an exact reproduction of a storybook, one page at a time. When a child touches one of the words displayed on the screen, the computer reads the word aloud, using a synchronized speech device. Touching a dot at the beginning of a line reads the whole line. Children can reread lines or change the sequence at will by touching the dots. Special boxes at the bottom of the screen let children flip pages forward or backward. The PERC project adapted several popular children's books to this format and provided teachers with an easy method for inserting stories dictated by the children.

The *Talking Page* activity is valuable because it heightens children's awareness that print conveys the story information. Touching a picture or some other portion of the screen does not produce speech. Because children can replay words and phrases many times, this activity helps reinforce the concept that words carry invariant meaning. The ability to control the story by touching different lines keeps the student actively involved in the book.

Unfortunately, PERC's *Talking Page* has not been replicated on many computer systems other than PLATO because it requires a tremendous amount of speech and a touch-sensitive screen. Both of these are expensive additions to a computer system. The speech production device used in this project was only minimally reliable. Nevertheless, the *Talking Page* remains an intriguing example of what is possible. Interactive video could reduce the cost of providing high-quality pictures and accurate oral reading while increasing mechanical reliability.

Texas Instruments' *Magic Wand Books* are an update of the *Talking Page* concept. These children's books add bar-code stripes across the bottom of each page. When a child slides a bar-code reader (magic wand) over the stripes, a computer-controlled speech synthesizer reads the page aloud. The use of bar codes avoids the speech production errors encountered in the original PLATO activity.

Songs and Nursery Rhymes

Children's songs and nursery rhymes use a highly predictable structure that appeals to young children. The repetition of key sounds and the use of simple melodies help young children to learn the rhymes quickly. These songs and rhymes introduce print by directing children's attention to the words and sounds in them.

Nursery Time and *Micro Mother Goose* are two examples of software that introduce reading through rhymes and simple songs. In *Nursery Time*, children select a rhyme by pressing any key, while in *Micro Mother Goose*, they move a cursor to the appropriate item. After a selection is made, both programs draw a picture based on the rhyme and play the song while displaying the lyrics on the screen (see Fig. 3.2).

The melodies created evade the shortcomings of synthetic speech because many small computers can play musical notes without difficulty. Children easily recognize the songs and remember the lyrics, and many enjoy singing along to the tune.

Nursery-rhyme software are very enjoyable, but the current versions would be more effective for reading readiness if they were more interactive and highlighted each word as it was played. After the initial selection, a child sits passively while the computer draws the illustration and plays the song. Interactive components easily could be added to these rhymes. For instance, the child presses a key whenever the song comes to a word containing a particular letter or sound to capture words for a prize box

Fig. 3.2   Screen from *Micro Mother Goose.*

Source: Reproduced with permission of Software Productions Inc.

occupying a corner of the screen. This game would draw attention to the song lyrics and assure a strong association between the spoken word and its printed form.

Personalized Books

Personalized books can increase a child's interest in a story. These use word-processing technology to incorporate aspects of the child's background into a personalized story book (see Fig. 3.3). The current models customize superficially, inserting only the child's name, address, and the names of parents, friends, and pets into the narrative. All were designed primarily for mail-order businesses where nothing else is known about the child. Nevertheless, computer technology has no intrinsic limitations to prohibit greater personalization. A program that encourages a teacher to insert additional personal information, thereby creating books that are more closely tied to a child's background experience, might be more educationally relevant.

LEARNING THE ALPHABET

Learning to identify the name of letters and their associated sounds is the most popular reading readiness activity. Knowledge of the alphabet is widely accepted as a measure of reading readiness and is taught in nearly all readiness programs, including those that also use computer-based instruction.

The *Talking Typewriter*

The earliest approach to alphabet learning is the Edison Responsive Environment Project, better known as the *Talking Typewriter*. This innovative device was first developed in 1960 by O. K. Moore. At its simplest level, the *Talking Typewriter* prints letters using large type and pronounces both the sound and the name of any letter pressed.

Initially, children are free to explore the typewriter's keys without adult interference. This "free typing" stage continues until the child tires of it. At this point, roles are reversed and the computer asks the child to locate a certain letter. The computer helps the student by ignoring all but

THAT'S WHAT HAPPENED TO JIMMY WHEN HE CHASED HIS MOUSE, MICKEY, ALONG MEADOW LANE AND TOWARD THE PLAYGROUND AT THE PARK WHERE ERIC, MARK AND JONATHAN WERE PLAYING.

JIMMY RAN AS FAST AS HE COULD, BUT MICKEY STAYED FAR AHEAD. JIMMY CAUGHT UP JUST AS MICKEY SLIPPED THROUGH THE DOOR OF A SHINING SPACESHIP.

"MICKEY, YOU COME OUT OF THERE," JIMMY SHOUTED, AND HE RACED IN AFTER THE MOUSE.

Fig. 3.3 Sample page from a personalized story book.

Source: Reprinted with permission of Creative Concepts Corporation. Ferne Arfin O'Shea, Adventures on the Riddle Planet *(Creative Concepts Corporation; Andover, MA, 1978),* p. 2.

the correct response and by illuminating the correct key with small lights under the keyboard. Again, children are free to experiment with various keys while searching for the correct one. When the child locates it, the computer repeats the letter name and sound and displays it on a large screen. After mastering all the letters, the child learns to type words in similar fashion. At the most advanced levels, children read and write long stories on the computer and use their newly acquired typing skills to produce a rudimentary newspaper (see Fig. 3.4). Throughout the sessions, children control the computer interaction and can choose to return to a simpler level whenever they want.

Developers of the *Talking Typewriter* interpret incorrect student responses not as errors, but as indications of a child's search strategies. Moore cautioned his assistants against providing prompts or other aids to children searching for a particular key. He reports that many children enjoy the freedom to experiment. The fundamental difference between this approach and that of conventional computer-based drills is best summarized by its creator, O. K. Moore:

> The Talking Typewriter is a *responsive device*. . . . An early example of a simple responsive device is the lyre. One does not ask how efficient a lyre is, as if it were a lever or a pulley; one does not ask about a lyre's fidelity as if it were a reproducer, say a phonograph. Instead, the kinds of questions one should ask about a lyre and the Talking Typewriter, too, are: "Do they foster emotional-cognitive growth?" "Are they fun to 'play' with?" What I am suggesting is that whereas most of those concerned with computers two decades ago conceived of them as highly efficient and faithful master clerks, we were trying to show their potential for enhancing human growth, especially the kind of growth that arises out of playfulness (Moore, 1980).

The creative synthesis of visual, auditory, and manual cues, along with emphasis on student control of the learning environment, make the *Talking Typewriter* unusual among computer-based instruction systems. Few reading programs allow a child to play with letters and words while also providing rich feedback based on the child's responses.

Evaluation studies by Moore and his associates showed that the *Talking Typewriter* was highly effective for introducing reading to diverse groups of children. After using the *Talking Typewriter* for only four months, "disadvantaged" kindergarten children increased their reading ability by

FURRY AND NUTTY
by Venn Moore

Once upon a time there were two
squirrels named Furry and Nutty.
They were very cute squirrels; they
would scamper up and down the trees
to play. Also they would do cute
tricks on telephone wires. These
squirrels liked acorns, peanuts and
walnuts. At night they hunted for
food and dug a hole to store it in
a secret place. They lived in holes
in trees; sometimes they moved away
to build a different kind of home.
One spring they had a baby and
named it Bushy. The reason they
wanted to name it Bushey was that
they lived in bushy trees and they
had bushy tails.
One day when they were doing tricks
on the telephone wires, it was
stormy and it lighteninged. It
caught on to the wire, and Furry was
electrocuted. Poor Furry was dead!
Poor Bushy and Nutty were alone.
From that time Nutty and Bushy were
more careful than they used to be.

TWO FIRES
by Jeffrey Batter

Once when we were going to school,
there was a fire on Laurel Road.
When the fire started, the children
were already outside, and the mother
was badly hurt. On March 31, my
brother lit a fire beside the garage.
The fireman next door put it out.

THE FUNNY BUNNY
by Shirley Horne

If I were a bunny,
I'd be funny.
I'd earn money.
By selling honey.
In the sunny
It would get all runny.
Isn't that funny?

THE PEABODY MUSEUM
by Mary Ellen Burns

During vacation I went to the
Peabody Museum with my Daddy
and my brother, Joseph. We saw
a big dinosaur, and it was so big
that Joseph had to look up. In the
same room we saw the largest turtle
in the whole wide world.

OUR TRIP TO BOSTON
by Lisa Whitcomb

We went to Boston and when we were
driving we had to stop to have
supper. We stayed with some friends.
When we got there, it was ten o'-
clock-- way past our bedtime.
We woke up Mom and bothered her.
I mostly watched TV. Daddy watched
TV with me, and Mom talked with
Ellie Priess. When Daddy was not
watching TV, he was talking to Uncle
Al. We had fun!

MY LOOSE TOOTH
by Kathy Johnstone

I have a loose tooth and it is my
first one. When it come out I will
put it in a glass of water and in
the morning I will find a quarter
under my pillow.
The fairy will leave the money for
me. I may buy some groceries with
it for my mother.

THE WOODPECKER
by Tamara Plakins

I saw somebody peck
And did wreck,
But I never saw anybody smack
Someone in the back.

Fig. 3.4 *A sample student newspaper.*

Source: O. J. Harvey, Experience Structure and Adaptability *(Springer Publishing Co.: New York, 1966), pp. 181–82. Reprinted with permission of O. J. Harvey.*

The boys and girls in Kindergarten are one year younger than we are.
They all made up their stories, and then they typed them for our
newspaper. We showed them how to cut a stencil. "Lab Record" Editors.

THE ELEPHANT
by Spencer Taylor

Once upon a time in the far away
land lived a little elephant named
Timmy. He ran away. He almost got
run over.

THE HAUNTED HOUSE
by Susan Connelly

The haunted house has ghosts and
goblins and demons. It's scarey to
go in, and you might get killed.

SUSAN SQUIRTED ME
by Pam Malley

My friend Susan squirted me with
water on my new dress. Susan had to
put her head down.

MY BIRTHDAY
by Richard Wright

May 3 is my birthday. I will blow
out the candles on my birthday cake.
I want a fire engine.

MOTHER
by Helen Greenspan

Mother is well now. The cast is
off her leg. Now she can drive me
to school. I am glad.

SOLDIERS
by Jonathan Cahn

This is fun. We play combat
soldiers. Davie and Stevie break
through our team. We break through
their team.

The Nursery school children just started to type their stories for the
"Lab Record" and we helped them type the stencils. The Editors.

PAM
by Melanie Canadeo

Pam, you could be a nurse some-
day. But when you be a nurse, you
can not scream like you do now.

A MONKEY
by Brian Symmes

I saw a monkey feeding peanuts
to lots of people.

I LIKE SCHOOL
by Carissa Whitcomb

I paint at Sharon's house. I
like Ricky. I like God. He makes us
healthy.

FISHING
by Larry Batter

I went fishing with my Father and
my brother and we caught a goldfish
and a whale!

PIRATES
by Charles Stainton

Larry and Charles are pirates.
When my baby brother sleeps, my
sister and I play outside.

Kites
by David Black

I went to the ball field and flew
kites. We didn't get to stay long.

Fig. 3.4 *(Continued)*

1.5 grade levels. In another study, participants learned to read new words 30 percent faster than students in conventional programs. Moore himself wrote a case study of a gifted but emotionally disturbed boy, suggesting that significant emotional growth can parallel a child's academic improvement.

The *Talking Typewriter* attracted much attention when it was first developed and, despite its high cost, was used in a variety of school and community settings. It was the first computer-based reading project to receive wide exposure in textbooks on reading methods. In recent years, however, the *Talking Typewriter* seems to have gone out of fashion, although its operation can be replicated on most small computers at a substantially lower cost. Perhaps student control of the learning process was and still is too radical a concept for computer curriculum developers.

Letter Identification Programs

Most commercial programs that introduce the letters of the alphabet require the student to press the key matching a large letter displayed on a screen. Some add to the challenge by mixing uppercase and lowercase letters, while others provide pictures to reinforce correct selections. Because of the inadequacies of computer-based speech, few programs teach the letter sound or name along with its visual form. Without an auditory component, these drills consist of little more than matching a shape on the screen to its corresponding key and thus fail to teach the phonemic role of letters in reading and writing. Because letters represent sounds, audio output is essential for computer programs that introduce the alphabet.

Discrimination among letters of the alphabet is a critical component of letter identification instruction. Studies in experimental psychology show that instruction is more efficient when students are taught the visual features that distinguish one letter from another. The three principal distinctive features of letters are curve, line, and angle. *Ball-Stick-Bird*, a noncomputerized initial reading program developed by Renee Fuller, is the only commercial curriculum that incorporates these three distinctive features directly into letter-recognition instruction. This program uses cardboard manipulatives to show children how each letter is formed by combining the basic shapes of ball, stick, and bird.

Ball-Stick-Bird is not well known, and few studies have been undertaken to evaluate its effectiveness. Pilot experiments show that four-year-olds learn to read more easily by this method and that older, low-readiness, handicapped children also benefit from its use. It demonstrates how abstract perceptual features can be made accessible to young children.

Fostering awareness of distinctive features by encouraging their manipulation lends itself well to a variety of computer activities. In the following hypothetical example, children move the distinctive features across a color video screen using simple switches or a sturdy joystick. Once the child has formed the letter from the distinctive features, animation slowly fuses the parts into a well-formed letter, while providing audio commentary about the letter's name, sound, and salient features (see Fig. 3.5).

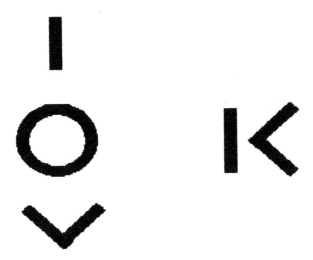

Fig. 3.5 A proposed activity for teaching letter formation modeled after the *Ball-Stick-Bird* curriculum.

Window Letters, part of the PLATO Early Reading Curriculum Project, illustrates another way of introducing the distinctive features of letters. This computer activity masks a large image of a letter behind a screen. Children peek at various parts of the letter by moving a small window on the screen until they are ready to guess the letter. This transforms letter recognition into an enjoyable and challenging game, prompting children to think about the visual elements that form individual letters. The original PLATO activity uses a window of fixed size to reveal letter parts. Using a variable size window that uncovers whole distinctive features could make this activity even more effective for teaching letter recognition.

Making Letters Familiar to Children

Letters and their associated sounds are abstract entities, foreign to the background experience of many children. Some psycholinguists argue that a child's inexperience with thinking about sounds independent of their underlying messages may cause certain types of reading difficulties. Learning is faster and easier when children are given tools to conceptualize sounds.

The *Alpha-Land* curriculum uses an unusually creative approach to this problem through conventional media. *Alpha-Land* converts each letter into a person whose characteristics emphasize the sound of the letter. Thus, "Mr. T," a large inflatable doll, carries a toothbrush and has a broad toothy smile. All his stories and songs emphasize words beginning with the letter "T." While this curriculum has proven to be an effective approach to initial reading, its heavy use of books, phonograph records, tapes, inflatable dolls, and other media makes the program very cumbersome for many classrooms. The versatility of computer displays, particularly interactive video systems, could simplify this program considerably.

The "Sesame Street" show developed by Children's Television Workshop has made letters familiar to children through clever animations in which a letter is transformed into a related word or object and back again. These special effects are impossible with conventional classroom media, but quite feasible on television. The fundamental flaw of television, however, is its passivity. Children can only watch and listen. Computer-controlled interactive video makes possible a diversity of alphabet games based on these special effects. At present, such programs are not available to schools, although activities based on the ideas introduced in *Alpha-Land* and "Sesame Street" could easily be adapted to computer-based interactive video.

BUILDING AN INITIAL READING VOCABULARY

Introducing children to an initial reading vocabulary is a self-evident aspect of all readiness programs. In typical prereading programs, children start by learning to read their own names, the names of their classmates, and other common words. Several computer activities have been developed to aid in this process.

CARIS uses computer animation to introduce the meaning of simple noun-verb sentences formed by students. At its simplest level of operation, children select words through the scanning procedure described on pages 44–45. Once the child has chosen a noun-verb combination, the computer generates a cartoon depicting the meaning of the sentence formed (see Fig. 3.6).

At advanced levels of *CARIS*, children are introduced to typing through a procedure similar to that of the *Talking Typewriter*. After they have

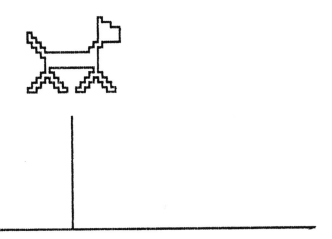

THE DOG JUMPS

Fig. 3.6 *CARIS* animation screen.

selected a word, *CARIS* guides their typing efforts to reproduce the word by ignoring all incorrect keystrokes. Children are free to try several keys as they search for the correct letter.

CARIS is intended primarily for low-readiness handicapped children in special education programs. Children at a developmental age as low as 2.5 years can learn to read and type the vocabulary and enjoy the game format of creating cartoons. The system is particularly useful for children with limited language proficiency caused by deafness or other communication handicaps.

CARIS builds on ideas similar to the *Talking Typewriter*. It creates a play environment where children can explore the meaning of simple sentences. Teachers are discouraged from prompting students to search for specific noun-verb combinations and from judging their responses. Externally imposed goals are unnecessary because children willingly set their own goals as they search for particular words. Children using *CARIS* frequently practice words and scold themselves when they make an unwanted selection. Indeed, the freedom to make mistakes without outside intervention is one of the strengths of exploratory-learning activities.

In its present form, *CARIS* is not a total reading curriculum. The variety of nouns and verbs available in this program is severely limited by the computer's inability to generate complex cartoons rapidly. The current model provides only twelve nouns and thirteen verbs. As the quality of display devices improves, increased vocabulary may be more feasible. Cartoons stored on videodisk, for example, could make available several dozen nouns and verbs.

The *DOVACK* system adopts a different approach. This program was designed to augment experience charts commonly used in kindergartens, particularly those that use the language experience approach. In *DOVACK*, children dictate stories to a teacher or aide who types them into a computer. The computer then provides a neatly typed copy of the story for the student, followed by an alphabetical list of all the words in the story. It also serves as a teacher resource, maintaining a log of the stories and all the words used by each student. The teacher can use these word lists to compose weekly vocabulary tests.

The word banks used in many reading-readiness classrooms can be adapted easily to a computer. As children encounter new words, the teacher can store them on disk in personally identified files, along with the child's definition of the word and perhaps a picture of its meaning. This word bank then becomes the center for diverse spelling and reading activities. A child could ask for all the words containing a particular letter combination, or for all those containing a certain key word in their definition. The word bank could even serve as a writing aid by allowing the child to check the spelling of new words rapidly. Computer word banks are particularly appropriate for remedial students because using a computer reduces the likelihood that older, nonreading students might perceive the word bank as "babyish."

DEVELOPING LANGUAGE COMPREHENSION

Reading is fundamentally a language activity. As such, any readiness instruction that increases children's ability to understand the language by increasing their vocabulary, syntactic skills, and information base also increases their reading readiness. This is particularly important at the preschool and kindergarten levels, where language skills are not fully developed.

Few language comprehension software have been designed for the readiness levels. Comprehension activities are not a major part of most computer-based reading curricula until the middle elementary years. This is a critical lack, in view of the considerable language growth that takes place in the early elementary years. Young children, particularly those with culturally diverse backgrounds, urgently need to improve all aspects of their language skills.

Many preschoolers have a poor understanding of relational terms such as "on," "under," "over," and "beside." The *Crane Game* could provide them with an enjoyable means of experimenting with these relational terms. In this computer program, objects are moved on a video screen using sentences such as "Put the red block under the green one." The computer parses the sentence and executes the desired actions.

The computer program underlying this activity is often an assigned project in computer-science courses on artificial intelligence because of the programming subtleties it requires. To teach relational terms to preschoolers, it simply needs a more suitable input system, which might rely on a cursor control to select items without the necessity for typing them. For example, a young child moves the cursor to the first object and presses any key on the keyboard. The computer responds by displaying the first part of the command:

Place the red block

The computer then presents a group of relational terms such as "over", "under", "in", "on", "beside", and "inside", that the child chooses by moving the cursor (see Fig. 3.7). A second object selection completes the sentence. The computer displays the resulting sentence at the bottom of the screen, and an animation executes its meaning.

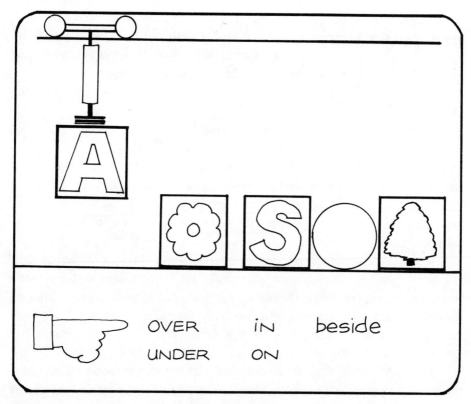

Fig. 3.7 *Crane Game* screen, a proposed activity for teaching relational terms.

STATE OF THE ART

Relatively few commercial reading programs are intended for readiness-level instruction. What does exist is often dominated by letter-matching drills and tutorials that introduce the keyboard. More creative applications have been tried, but few are available commercially.

Readiness instruction is inherently the most difficult reading domain to computerize. When a child is unable to read text from the screen or printer and is unable to type, the interaction options are severely limited. The most creative readiness programs use pictures, animation, and special input techniques to reinforce beginning reading skills. Some of these new devices, such as interactive video, increase the cost of a computer. At present, most innovation in reading-readiness software is taking place in special education, where expensive equipment is more clearly cost effective.

Exploratory-learning approaches are particularly important for readiness-level instruction. When young children learn to read in a game format that they can control, they engage more readily in the learning process. Activities like the *Talking Typewriter* and *CARIS* demonstrate that even very young children and low-readiness handicapped children can acquire initial reading skills in this manner.

Word Identification **4**

I can read. . . .
I just don't know the words.
—a first grader

Word identification is one of the most visible aspects of reading. Despite the child's assertion above, few people would claim that reading is possible without it. Nevertheless, word identification is merely a tool that facilitates reading comprehension, which is the central purpose of reading.

Word identification is the most popular type of computer-based reading activity. Drills, spelling games, and similar practice lessons are easy to program on most small computers. While many such programs exist, most of them lack a solid basis in the current reading instruction theories.

SKILLED WORD IDENTIFICATION

Word identification includes two closely related components: translating the printed symbols into speech sounds and recognizing those sounds as meaningful words. These two skills are tightly interlinked because meaning is frequently a potent aid for determining the sound of a letter string, while sounding out the letters is a technique often used to determine meaning.

Word identification may be compared with walking. With the exception of certain special functions, such as modeling or formal processions, the elegance of a person's gait matters less than the ability to move from one point to another. Indeed, the stylized gait of a fashion model would prove very tiring on a hike or a trip to the post office.

Similarly, except for dramatic readings, formal addresses, or other public speeches, word identification is a utilitarian tool used to facilitate comprehension. Few adults are regularly called upon to read aloud or demonstrate word identification outside an academic setting. The important skills for adult readers are their ability to understand what they read and to relate that information to their personal and professional lives.

Walking is deceptively simple and, for most people, automatic. With the exception of toddlers and severely handicapped individuals, few people need to think consciously about coordinating the muscles used in walking; even fewer can identify the muscles involved. Walking is automatic, demanding conscious attention only when a person is faced with a dangerous situation such as traversing a narrow ledge or slippery surface. For most of the time, the walker is free to consider other matters.

For skilled readers word identification is also a spontaneous task. Most readers report that individual words appear to them as whole entities, with no discernable effort on their part. Few people are aware of the complex processes that take place during word identification. Only when confronted with an unfamiliar word does the reader think about its pronunciation or identity.

This automatic aspect of word identification may be particularly important, because many cognitive psychologists believe that humans have only a finite supply of conscious attention. As more effort is diverted toward word identification, less attention remains for understanding the ideas in a passage. Automatic word identification liberates a reader to devote full attention to comprehension. However, recent research shows that, while automatic word recognition may be necessary for good comprehension, it is not sufficient. A child may still need instruction in comprehension skills to understand a topic.

Automatic word recognition is the product of extensive practice in the reading of text. Just as toddlers must concentrate to walk, beginning readers must devote much attention to decoding the words in the text. While instruction in word identification subskills may be pedagogically convenient, fluent word identification comes primarily through experience in reading words and stories.

Word Identification Cues

Word identification involves the flexible use of diverse skills. Phonics is the best-known of these skills, although several others are equally important. The following example illustrates the richness of word identification cues available to a sophisticated reader:

> All that summer, Joe and Rick were inseparable. They played together every day and even attended the same summer camp.

If a reader does not know the word "inseparable," this passage provides abundant cues to unlock both its meaning and pronunciation.

- *Syntactic cues.* The sentence grammar suggests that this word is a name for a person, place, or condition.
- *Semantic cues.* The passage structure suggests that the second sentence elaborates on the first one. "Inseparable" seems to relate to the two boys doing everything together.
- *Structural analysis cues.* The letters "i-n" look like a prefix for "not," while "able" may be a suffix, suggesting that the two boys are "not something able." If the two boys are always together, perhaps this word means they are not able to be parted.
- *Syllabication cues.* Because the pronunciation of the two affixes is well known, only the root needs further attention. The core "separ" looks as though it could be divided into two syllables "se" and "par."
- *Phonic cues.* Each of these two syllables can now be pronounced using standard letter-sound correspondences. Afterwards, the prefixes and suffixes are reattached to form the full word.

This example is not meant to suggest that readers must consciously analyze all available word identification cues for every word in a story, but rather that they may use a diversity of information when attempting to identify an unknown word. In reality, the reader uses the minimum information needed to identify the word and proceeds with the story.

The example illustrates the centrality of meaning in word identification. In some situations, once meaning is recognized, further attention to the word may not be necessary. When reading foreign terms in a text, some readers never learn the correct pronunciation. Even in academic contexts, when correct pronunciation is required, readers attend to meaning to identify recognizable affixes, thereby simplifying the phonic analysis demands.

Instructional Goals for Word Identification

1. *Provide students with frequent and varied practice.* Students may need several encounters with a word in varied settings before they learn the word. Reading a word only once or twice is rarely effective.

2. *Emphasize the use of all available cues.* Words are learned by forming strong associations with other words and ideas. Word identification instruction is most effective when it considers all relevant phonic, structural, and contextual elements, as well as the word's spelling and meaning.

3. *Develop awareness of the internal structure.* The spelling and phonic patterns in words can provide students with tools to identify new vocabulary.

4. *Develop automatic word identification strategies.* Students master a word only when they can read it quickly and without giving conscious attention to word identification.

5. *Introduce vocabulary in a story context.* Prose provides valuable word identification cues for identifying new vocabulary. In addition, the introduction of new words in a text encourages students to apply their word identification skills to everyday reading tasks.

COMPUTER IMPLEMENTATIONS

Word identification instruction has become the most popular domain for computer-based reading programs. Unfortunately, current commercial offerings are dominated by programs that overemphasize phonic and spelling cues without comparable concern for the role of meaning in word identification. These programs deprive students of important semantic and discourse cues.

Activities Involving Isolated Words

Tachistoscope or Flash Card Programs.   These present a letter or word on a screen for a short period of time. Typically, a child watches for a word flashed for about one second and then picks the word from among several distractors. Emphasis is placed on practicing rapid identification of new vocabulary through what amounts to computerized flash cards.

Flash card programs are easy to write, particularly when precise presentation timing is not critical. A typical BASIC program can be less than one page long. Sample flash card programs are frequently published in anthologies of BASIC computer programs.

Flash card programs are popular with children who enjoy the challenge of speed. While the children gain practice in the rapid recognition of words, these activities do little to draw their attention to the internal structure of the word or its use in prose. Children who work primarily with word lists sometimes learn to recognize a word through idiosyncratic features. A beginner might learn to recognize the word "elephant" as "the long word" in a flash card set. Such cues cannot be transferred to reading the word in other environments.

Word Search Puzzles.   A favorite leisure-time word identification activity, these puzzles embed a list of words in a matrix of random letters. Words appear horizontally, vertically, or diagonally. Children as well as adults enjoy these games, which are thought to improve spelling and word identification skills.

An assortment of computer programs are capable of generating word search puzzles automatically. Most of these are easy to use and are intended as aids to printing the puzzles on paper. The teacher types a list of target words into the computer, and, in a matter of seconds, the computer produces a copy of the puzzle on a printer in a format ready for duplication. The computer even prints a key to the puzzle for later checking. More sophisticated versions permit children to solve the puzzle directly on the video terminal instead of on paper.

The actual reading benefit of word search puzzles remains uncertain because of the substantial difference between these puzzles and normal prose. Reading a story does not require the recognition of words printed in strange orientations without spaces between them. Some children, especially those labeled "perceptually handicapped" or "distractible," find the activities very frustrating because of the visual overload these puzzles create.

Spelling Games.   Traditionally considered a part of the writing curriculum, spelling games are also useful for word identification purposes because they make students more aware of a word's internal structure. Word identification programs are most successful when they combine reading with the spelling of a new word.

Some computer-based spelling games use word scrambles. These present a word with its letters in scrambled order on a video screen and challenge a student to correct the spelling using the computer keyboard. More complex computer programs award bonus points to students who unscramble a word rapidly.

Pencil-and-paper versions of word scramble are already widely accepted, and computerized versions of these games can offer few additional benefits. While computers do increase student interest in these games, this may not be the best use of limited computer resources.

Combinatorial Games.   Students are presented with two or more lists containing word parts and combine parts from each list to create whole words. This activity is particularly suited for teaching affixes and compound words. Britannica's *Fragmentation* game illustrates some of the advantages of computerized versions of combinatorial games. The participants can direct the computer to display clues and move the cursor to build a word from the parts. When a correct word is formed, the computer merges the two parts and displays a definition of the word (see Fig. 4.1). A time limit adds challenge to the activity, while the clues provide information about the meaning of each fragment and word.

Phonics Drills.   These give students practice focusing on the sound-symbol regularities. Because most inexpensive computer systems can neither produce accurate speech nor assess a child's utterances, they rely on non-oral phonics instruction.

One method displays a picture on a video screen along with four letters, one of which represents the beginning sound of the picture's name.

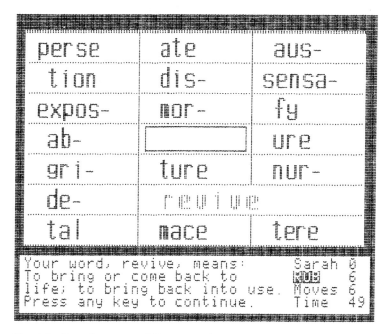

Fig. 4.1 Sample screen of *Fragmentation*.
Source: Reprinted with permission of Encyclopaedia Britannica.

This reduces phonics to matching a picture label with its initial letter and works adequately, provided the pictures are sufficiently unambiguous.

Sound-matching activities use a similar approach to non-oral phonics instruction. In these, the student picks from a group of words the one containing the same sound as a target word. This paradigm can be used for practicing initial word sounds, medial vowel sounds, ending sounds, or rhymes. However, it is important that these matching activities truly be sound-matching and cannot be solved merely by finding a word that shares the same letters as the target word. When letter similarity alone suffices, the activity's value for phonics instruction is greatly diminished.

An example of visually matched words:

1. FIND THE WORD THAT ENDS WITH THE SAME SOUND AS
                    MOUSE
          MATCH   HOUSE   CHAIR

An example of phonetically matched words:

2. FIND THE WORD THAT ENDS WITH THE SAME SOUND AS
BABY
TREE   FLY   BIKE

In another kind of drill, a reader is asked to discriminate between alternative sounds for a given letter, such as long and short vowel sounds. Being able to classify the two sounds can be helpful but is not essential to fluent reading. In fact, most readers identify the sound *after* they have read the word. Thus, phoneme classification is a product of word identification rather than a helpful aid. Some adults who were educated in schools that did not emphasize phonics have reported that they learned these distinctions only after helping their own children with phonics homework.

While computer-based word identification programs frequently include these phonics activities, most have serious limitations. Many programs are direct imitations of workbook activities. Aside from the immediate reinforcement of correct responses, the computer contributes little that is unavailable in printed form at substantially lower cost. Moreover, these programs teach word identification as though it consisted of little more than memorizing arbitrary letter strings, much like learning a set of telephone numbers. They ignore the rich meaning of words in natural language and overlook important cues such as context and semantics. A few superficially include them by embedding the word in a sentence. A word scramble activity might provide clues in the form of a sentence with the target word deleted:

SDIWHSEANC

THE CHILDREN ATE _____FOR LUNCH.

While this simple use of context provides meaning and language cues in word identification, a more radical approach could fully integrate word identification with meaning.

Instant Phonics illustrates a creative approach to computer-based phonics instruction. This program is in the form of a game played by two participants trying to discover the identity of a word spelled phonetically. Students take turns and may guess the word or request clues that give information

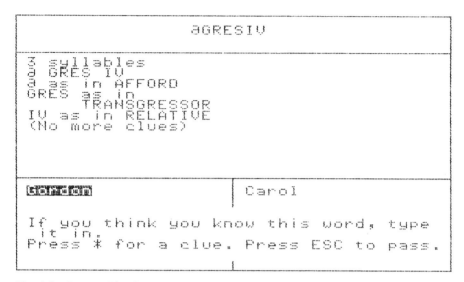

Fig. 4.2 *Instant Phonics.* An experimental word identification game by Intentional Educations, Inc.

about the word's pronunciation, syllabication, definition, and use in simple sentences (See Fig. 4.2). Points are awarded to the first student who correctly spells the word. This game encourages children to consider multiple cues in word identification.

Instant Phonics, however, has one problem: it presents a phonetically spelled word and challenges students to guess its standard spelling. As such, it is actually the inverse of reading, where students see the standard spelling and must deduce its pronunciation. Because the program provides a convenient editor for inserting new items, it is easy to reconstruct the activity to parallel reading more closely. For example, children might look at a correctly spelled word and guess its phonetic spelling, with the computer providing helpful clues as before.

WORD IDENTIFICATION IN THE FUTURE

As small computers become more sophisticated, word identification lessons will grow in complexity. While these could take the form of more elaborate word drills, an approach that models efficient use of all cues in a prose context is preferable. Students would thus gain expertise in all word identification cues, and the similarity of these lessons to normal text would assure that they transfer their word identification skills to other reading material.

The Components

Speech Production.   Speech production by computer is an important aspect of future word identification lessons. The current lack of fully adequate speech production has forced curriculum developers to use unwieldy substitutes for audio output. When a child needs assistance in pronouncing an unfamiliar word, a computer program that can say the word is a better educational tool than a pronunciation guide such as the following:

PLASMA

1. PL   AS IN "<u>PL</u>AY"
2. AS   AS IN "<u>AS</u>"
3. MA   AS IN "<u>MUH</u>"

While synchronized speech devices have adequate tonal quality, their low reliability makes them unsuitable for most word identification instruction. Synthesized speech is more reliable and versatile, but the tonal quality of current models is inadequate for instruction in word pronunciation. With the development of new, inexpensive speech synthesizers, better vocal accuracy will be available in the near future.

Speech Recognition.   Speech recognition by computer would be an enormous asset for word identification instruction. A computer programmed to listen to a student reading aloud could evaluate for accuracy and immediately remediate word identification difficulties. However, current automated voice recognition is crude and too expensive for schools. Many businesses are researching office machines capable of transcribing speech into print without human intervention. As these become commercially available, they should offer exciting possibilities for reading instruction.

Video Displays.   These use space more dynamically than conventional print media. High-resolution video terminals, similar to those already used in commercial and industrial environments, make possible the display of long segments of text that can be read without undue eyestrain. Portions of a screen can be overlayed with additional information as needed. For example, a student could instruct the computer to display a word's definition inside a window at the bottom of the screen, followed by information about the word's etymology and pronunciation. To resume reading, the student need only press a special key. Such display techniques would make available a broad range of word identification resources.

A Lesson of the Near Future

Chris is in a sixth-grade reading class. Today she is practicing her word identification skills using a book that the class is reading. She sits at a computer terminal that is equipped with a high-resolution screen capable of displaying a full page of text, along with illustrations and colored backgrounds. The first page of her text looks like this:

It had seemed like an exciting adventure last summer when he decided to take up residence on Parker Mountain. But now things were different. The snow crunched under Jim's feet as he slowly climbed the trail up the mountainside to his cabin. Even the woollen scarf wrapped around his face offered little protection against the north wind. He glanced up at the early evening sky already ablaze with stars: it would be a cold night, he thought. The bitter wind even bothered Spiro who now stayed close to the path with head and tail low. Spiro usually enjoyed these daily treks, scampering up and down the familiar trail and often stopping to inspect the fresh tracks of a snowshoe rabbit. Jim knew the cabin would be frigid by now, the fire in the woodstove having died out hours ago. He would have to restart it and keep it burning through the long night ahead to hold the temperature inside the cabin at a comfortable level. The uneasy thought now occurred to him, as it often did at such times, that his decision to rough it for a year had been a mistake after all.

Chris wants help with the word "residence." She uses a joystick connected to the computer to move the cursor, a flashing square of light, to the unknown word and presses the joystick's button. The computer creates a window over the bottom portion of the text, displaying a range of options:

It had seemed like an exciting adventure last summer when he decided to take up
residence on Parker Mountain. But now things were different. The snow crunched
under Jim's feet as he slowly climbed the trail up the mountainside to his cabin.
Even the woollen scarf wrapped around his face offered little protection against the
north wind. He glanced up at the early evening sky already ablaze with stars: it
would be a cold night, he thought. The bitter wind even bothered Spiro who now
stayed close to the path with head and tail low. Spiro usually enjoyed these daily
treks, scampering up and down the familiar trail and often stopping to inspect the
fresh tracks of a snowshoe rabbit. Jim knew the cabin would be frigid by now, the
fire in the woodstove having died out hours ago. He would have to restart it and

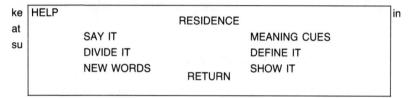

The computer is now ready to assist in recognizing the word with
a variety of options. The cursor appears in the window, allowing Chris
to select items in the same manner as before. If she chooses "say it",
the speech synthesizer pronounces the word and repeats it every time
she presses the button until she chooses another option.

The "new words" option adds this word to Chris's list of new vocabulary.
The computer uses this list to select items for spelling and word identification games. Words added to this list can be deleted when the student
has mastered their identification in a multitude of settings.

Selecting the option "divide it" causes the computer to provide assistance
in sounding out the word. This might take the following form:

fresh tracks of a snowshoe rabbit. Jim knew the cabin would be frigid by now, the
fire in the woodstove having died out hours ago. He would have to restart it and

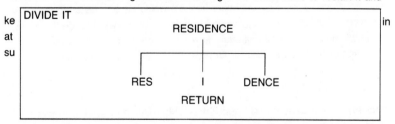

In this case the computer shows how the word is divided into syllables.
Synthetic speech pronounces each syllable individually, while a speech

recognition device monitors Chris's pronunciation. As the computer moves the letters closer together on the screen, the syllables blend until the original word is restored. If the word has useful affixes, these are indicated in similar fashion.

Chris is also free to look for relevant meaning cues or to read a definition of the word:

fresh tracks of a snowshoe rabbit. Jim knew the cabin would be frigid by now, the
fire in the woodstove having died out hours ago. He would have to restart it and

ke | DEFINE IT | in
at | RESIDENCE
su | THE PLACE WHERE SOMEONE LIVES OR KEEPS A HOME.
   | SIMILAR WORDS ARE: HOME, APARTMENT, HOUSE.
   | RETURN

When Chris is satisfied that she understands the new word, she moves the cursor to the word "return". This restores the screen to its initial state, allowing her to resume reading. Throughout her reading lesson, Chris can examine any word in the text. These digressions are not considered reading errors, nor is Chris penalized for slow or inadequate reading strategies.

Comprehension 5

The next class period is Michael's reading comprehension lesson. He checks his assignment sheet to confirm that lesson six is part of the day's assignment. He removes disk six from the file, slides it into the disk drive and turns on the computer. A few moments later, the computer displays the start of the lesson on the video screen:

WELCOME TO COMPREHENSION LESSON
NUMBER 6

WHAT IS YOUR FIRST NAME? **MICHAEL**

TODAY YOU WILL READ A STORY ABOUT CHARLES DREW, A FAMOUS BLACK DOCTOR. HIS WORK HELPED TO SAVE THE LIVES OF MANY PEOPLE DURING WORLD WAR II.

ARE YOU READY TO BEGIN? **YES**

The first page of the story appears on the video screen. Michael reads slowly and carefully. When he finishes, he presses the space bar to move to the second page. After he has read the second page, he is presented with the following questions:

WHAT WAS THE MAJOR AREA OF DR. DREW'S WORK?

1. HE PIONEERED BLOOD TRANSFUSION.
2. HE DEVELOPED MANY NEW DRUGS.
3. HE TRAINED YOUNG DOCTORS.

YOUR ANSWER IS: **1**

GOOD WORK!

WHAT IS "PLASMA"?

   1. AN IMPORTANT NEW DRUG.
   2. THE LIQUID PART OF BLOOD.
   3. A NEW TYPE OF SURGICAL TOOL.

YOUR ANSWER IS: **1**

   NO, THE ANSWER IS /// 2 ///.

WHAT DID DR. DREW DO TO HELP DURING THE WAR?

   1. HE FOUGHT BRAVELY IN EUROPE.
   2. HE ORGANIZED BLOOD DRIVES FOR WOUNDED SOLDIERS.
   3. HE SHOWED DOCTORS HOW TO CURE BATTLEFIELD DISEASES.

YOUR ANSWER IS: **2**

YOU ARE CORRECT!

After three more reading passages and several additional questions, Michael's assignment is completed. The computer displays the message:

MICHAEL, YOU ANSWERED 15 OUT OF 20 QUESTIONS CORRECTLY.

YOUR SCORE IS 75%.

PLEASE RECORD THIS SCORE ON YOUR DAILY ASSIGNMENT SHEET.

I HOPE WE WILL WORK TOGETHER AGAIN SOON.

GOODBYE.

Michael's hypothetical lesson is typical of many commercial reading comprehension programs and illustrates their limitations and weaknesses.

At first glance, lesson six seems to be well written. The information is presented succinctly, and Michael's score is calculated accurately. The computer's messages are clear and friendly. Yet, Michael's lesson might have been just as successful if he had used a pencil and paper. Indeed, the lesson is almost a direct transcription of workbook exercises. The immediate correction of errors is the only element unavailable in conventional media. Using a computer as an expensive workbook seems a waste of money and resources.

Closer inspection of Michael's lesson shows an arbitrary series of questions, most of which require him to remember explicit details from the story. Although the questions are unambiguous and clearly presented, they are based on what is convenient to ask rather than on a distinct model of reading comprehension. The overall concept of the lesson seems to be the premise that understanding a passage means being able to answer recall questions about the story's contents. This casts a reader into a passive role and ignores the reader's internal goals and experiences. It reduces reading to a memory contest, not an opportunity to reflect on the ideas in the passage.

Four key elements underlie comprehension of a passage:

- *Vocabulary.* Knowing the meaning of the words in a text.
- *Language skills.* Inferring meaning from the syntactic relationships among words in a text.
- *Schemata.* Applying prior knowledge to the reading task.
- *Manipulative skills.* Integrating the above comprehension elements appropriately.

While each of these elements is distinct and crucial for comprehension, they are interrelated, and weaknesses in one area can be partly balanced by strengths in another. Describing them as separate skills may be pedagogically convenient, but the proficient reader uses all four factors flexibly.

VOCABULARY DEVELOPMENT

Understanding the meaning of individual words used by a writer is the first component of reading comprehension. A reader may infer the meaning of some words from the surrounding context, but when too many words are unknown, full comprehension is impossible. Thus, while it is not necessary for the reader to master all words in a text, familiarity with the majority of words is needed for successful comprehension.

Vocabulary has both an extensive and an intensive component. Extensive vocabulary refers to the number of different words that a reader comprehends. Beyond the early elementary years, extensive vocabulary development often proceeds with the teaching of progressively rarer and more specialized terms. This skill is most frequently practiced in vocabulary items such as:

A DOMESTIC ANIMAL IS ONE THAT IS _____

1. SICK   3. TAME
2. OLD   4. WILD

Intensive vocabulary development is the study of multiple meanings of words. Unlike artificial codes, words in natural language usually have several meanings. This phenomenon is especially frequent among common words. Consider, for example, the diverse uses of the word "run":

I run home.
I run a business.
I hit a home run.
My nose runs.
I had a run of good luck.
There was a run at the bank.
I may run for president.
My stocking has a run.
Enter the run command into the computer.

Intensive vocabulary is easy to overlook. Nearly all young children appear to understand the word "run" and use it liberally in their speech. This may lead adults to infer that children understand all meanings of the word. In reality, young children typically understand only the most common interpretation of the word and may be confused by its less obvious uses. This is particularly true of idioms, figures of speech, and other abstract forms. Children's misinterpretations of commonly used expressions sometimes produce amusing anecdotes.

An Example of Confusions Caused by Figurative Language

A four-year-old boy overheard a conversation between his mother and his grandfather about how the grandfather had been forced to "fire" an insubordinate employee. For several days afterwards, the boy acted strangely toward his grandfather until he finally asked his mother "Why did grandfather shoot the man?"

Vocabulary Drills

Multiple-choice vocabulary drills seem to be the preferred instructional activity for computer-based vocabulary development. In these the reader must select the synonym for a target word from a group of words:

PICK THE WORD THAT MEANS THE SAME AS

ABUNDANT
  A. RARE
  B. PLENTIFUL
  C. ADEQUATE

This type of drill has several shortcomings. The repeated presentation of isolated words may lead a child to conclude that meanings lie in the words themselves. This ignores the intensive aspect of words, namely, that the meaning of most words is found only through attention to usage in sentence and story context. The following example, taken from the vocabulary strand of the Computer Curriculum Corporation's reading program, illustrates how context may be included in a vocabulary drill:

THE BOY WAS SCARED OF THE DARK.
WHEN THE LIGHTS WERE OUT, HE CROUCHED IN A CORNER.
WHEN YOU CROUCH IN A CORNER YOU MAKE YOURSELF AS _____ AS
POSSIBLE.

   SMALL   TALL   LARGE   LOUD

The CCC reading program also uses a different response format; the student types the word, and the computer recognizes misspellings. For example, when a student types "smal", the computer responds:

YOU MIGHT HAVE THE RIGHT ANSWER, BUT THE SPELLING IS WRONG. CHECK
THE SPELLING AND TYPE THE ANSWER AGAIN.

Spelling the word reinforces word identification cues and the word's meaning simultaneously. Unlike programs that evaluate incorrect spelling as a vocabulary error, the CCC reading program reduces that likelihood.

Activities such as these, however, still fail to make efficient use of computers. In effect, they are indistinguishable from traditional workbook exercises.

Word Processing for Vocabulary Development

Vocabulary instruction need not be limited to formal drills. Word processing operations can be the basis for innovative approaches to intensive vocabulary development, as illustrated in the following vignette:

The next period is Ralph Moffett's remedial English class. All ten of his fourth-grade students have English language deficiencies, of causes varying from foreign background to delayed development. This week, he is working on developing their appreciation of multiple meanings in words. Before class, he types the following text into his word processor:

After the game, Billy <u>runs</u> home. He tells his mother about the home <u>run</u> he hit for his team. The team now has a <u>run</u> of ten games without a single loss. If their <u>run</u> of good luck continues, they will be the best team in town.

Billy's mother says she is proud of him. At dinnertime, she tells him to <u>run</u> into the bathroom to wash. She tells him to be sure to <u>run</u> the water over his hands well to get all the dirt off. She also reminds him that tonight is his turn to clear the table and <u>run</u> the dishwasher.

Mr. Moffett gives a brief introductory lesson about the different meanings of words depending on how they are used in a story. Then he asks the students to read his story and think of a word that means the same as "run."

One girl suggests the word "race." Mr. Moffett types the following command:

REPLACE ALL LETTERS /RUN/ WITH /RACE/

In a few seconds, the text reappears as follows:

After the game, Billy <u>races</u> home. He tells his mother about the home <u>race</u> he hit for his team. The team now has a <u>race</u> of ten games without a single loss. If their <u>race</u> of good luck continues, they will be the best team in town.

Billy's mother says she is proud of him. At dinnertime, she tells him to <u>race</u> into the bathroom to wash. She tells him to be sure to <u>race</u> the water over his hands well to get all the dirt off. She also reminds him that tonight is his turn to clear the table and <u>race</u> the dishwasher.

The students read the revised story and, amid some laughter, discuss the suitability of each substitution. When they find a sentence in which "race" correctly replaces "run," Mr. Moffett types a command to mark the sentence in the computer. When the students have gone through the whole passage, he enters the commands:

UNDO THE LAST REPLACE.
LIST ALL MARKED SENTENCES AT END.

The following sentences appear at the end of the passage:

After the game, Billy runs home.
At dinnertime, she tells him to run into the bathroom to wash.

He finishes by inserting a remark before the two sentences:

RUN CAN MEAN *RACE* SOMETIMES.

The students investigate several other synonyms for "run." The capability of immediately testing each synonym in the text provides them with a strong stimulus for discussion on how to determine when a particular meaning applies. Reading the story at the end with all substitutions in place makes the vocabulary lesson concrete to the students.

The computer technology underlying this vocabulary lesson is available in most word processing software. Nearly all have the capacity to locate and replace words in a text and to copy marked sentences into a new location. This word processing capacity provides a powerful means of experimenting with synonyms for idioms, figures of speech, and technical vocabulary. Other approaches to teaching vocabulary can be devised by imaginative teachers, but drills are best left to pencil and paper.

DEVELOPING LINGUISTIC SKILLS

Sentence Grammar

"The car runs fast" is a meaningful sentence while "Fast runs car the" is nonsense. Reading the second example with normal intonation is difficult; most people would recite it like a list of individual words. Nearly all adults have a powerful intuitive understanding of sentence grammar. They generally recognize a well-formed sentence quickly and with remarkably uniform agreement among individuals.

Children begin to acquire grammatical skills early in life. First-graders understand and produce most sentences correctly, leading some adults to assume that children's grammatical development is virtually finished before they enter school. Recent research, however, indicates that sentence comprehension is far from complete at the preschool age and that it continues well into the elementary school years. Moreover, children with learning disabilities and other handicaps often show delayed development of grammatical skills.

Computer Applications

Drills displaying individual sentences on a screen are typical of computer-based instructional programs for teaching grammatical skills. In a drill, children may be asked to select which of several sentences is grammatically correct:

WHICH SENTENCE IS CORRECT:

1. NEITHER OF THE BOYS IS HERE.
2. NEITHER OF THE BOYS ARE HERE.
3. NEITHER OF THE BOYS IS NOT HERE.
4. NEITHER OF THE BOYS ARE NOT HERE.

Devising practice sentences based on particular grammatical structures and transformations is often a difficult and tedious task. Kirk Wilson and Madeleine Bates of the ILIAD Project at Bolt Beranek and Newman have developed a program that enables a computer to generate an unlimited number of sentences based on any specified series of syntactic patterns and transformations.

Reston Publishing's *Sentence Maker* illustrates how grammar lessons can be turned into a motivational game. In this program, two students compete to guess a famous saying from its initials. Points are awarded to the player who finds a correct word or guesses the entire saying (see Fig. 5.1).

At an advanced level of *Sentence Maker*, children take turns composing sentences that fit a five-initial sequence presented by the computer. Because they cannot use the same word in two different sentences, devising sentences that fit the pattern becomes progressively harder.

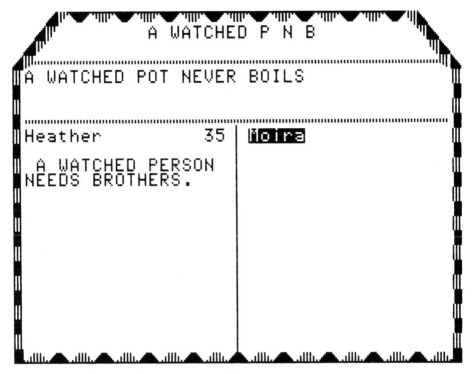

Fig. 5.1   Sample screen from *Sentence Maker*.

Several elements of this activity make it useful instructionally. Students enter guesses by typing a complete sentence, providing them with ample practice in sentence formation. Each student checks the grammar of an opponent's sentence; if students disagree, the computer pauses until agreement is reached. Words guessed correctly encourage students to use sentence context to infer the sentence's remaining words. Finally, scoring points makes this activity an enjoyable and challenging game.

Activities that focus on identifying correct surface grammars as in the drill above or inserting words into a preset surface form as in *Sentence Maker*, however, violate most current models of language and language development. Modern psycholinguists believe that children do not learn grammar by absorbing adult sentence patterns, but rather by gradually creating their own internal grammar. This personal grammar is initially different from standard English. Through continued experience, it gradually evolves into standard grammar. Children comprehend messages by parsing them according to their own current internal grammar. As a result, they sometimes think they understand a sentence when their interpretation is actually quite different from that of adults. Drills in the correct formation of isolated sentences are of little relevance to language acquisition.

Surface-grammar activities ignore meaning by treating grammar as a collection of abstract sentence patterns and transformations. Children use meaning as the principal cue for parsing sentences and are most likely to judge a sentence grammatically correct when they can infer a plausible meaning. Recent research on parent-child conversation shows that adults frequently correct meaningless phrases and incorrect information but ignore grammatical errors in semantically appropriate sentences. An approach based on meaning cues instead of surface grammar is more consistent with current thought on language acquisition. The following drill illustrates a meaning-based approach to teaching a structure such as the passive voice:

WHICH SENTENCE MEANS THE SAME AS:

AFTER FALLING OFF THE BICYCLE, THE BOY WAS COMFORTED BY THE GIRL.

A. THE BOY FELL OFF HIS BICYCLE AND THEN THE GIRL COMFORTED HIM.
B. THE GIRL FELL OFF HER BICYCLE AND COMFORTED THE BOY.
C. THE GIRL FELL OFF HER BICYCLE AND WAS COMFORTED BY THE BOY.
D. THE BOY FELL OFF HIS BICYCLE AND COMFORTED THE GIRL.

Meaning-centered drills, in which children encounter a well-formed sentence and must choose among several plausible interpretations, are more compatible with the task of reading comprehension. Surface-grammar drills resemble proofreading tasks and are more useful for writing instruction than for reading.

Surface-grammar drills also disregard the importance of the child as the central agent in language growth. Children need to experiment with grammar to discover its structure. These drills fail to give children a chance to observe the effect of different syntactic forms on the meaning of a sentence. Activities like the *Crane Game* described in Chapter 3 or *Eliza*, which will be described in Chapter 6, might provide a better framework for grammar instruction, because they permit children to manipulate sentences in playful ways. Unfortunately, few curriculum developers have adopted this approach because computer-based grammatical analysis is difficult to program.

The Cloze Procedure

All the language development activities described so far lack story context. Reading usually involves continuous stories, not isolated sentences. The cloze procedure is one of the most effective approaches for helping students improve their attention to linguistic cues as they read. In this activity, words are periodically omitted from the text and replaced by blank spaces. The reader must infer the missing word from the surrounding context.

Deleting every fifth word is the most frequently used cloze pattern. When using cloze for language instruction, teachers sometimes find it helpful to delete specific types of words. For example, the following passage draws attention to words that signal temporal organization:

TOMORROW, CATHY AND ALICE WILL TRAVEL TO OHIO TO VISIT THEIR GRANDMOTHER. THEY HAVE MANY THINGS TO DO _____ THEY LEAVE. _____, ALICE MUST FINISH ALL HER HOMEWORK; _____ SHE MUST PACK HER CLOTHES CAREFULLY. CATHY MUST GO TO THE TRAIN STATION _____ LUNCH TO BUY TICKETS. _____ THEY ARE READY, THEIR FATHER WILL DRIVE THEM TO THE STATION.

THEN	FIRST	WHEN	BEFORE	AFTER

The least radical computer-based cloze activities are programs that automate the production of cloze text. A teacher or aide uses word processing to enter text samples into a computer file. The cloze program then prints the text on paper with the deletions in place, accompanied by a list of the deleted words at the end of the text. A scoring key is also generated automatically. Students then complete the cloze passage as a pencil-and-paper task. More complex computer-based activities present the cloze materials directly on a video screen. Some programs use a multiple-choice response format, while others allow children to type the words in the correct spaces.

Because computer programs still have poor language processing features, the deletion of specific passage elements, such as the signal words for time sequence, must be done manually. Fortunately, the word-processing capacity of computers makes it easy to replace words with blank spaces.

Story Grammars

Story grammars are based on the premise that a well-constructed story follows a distinct series of stages. Omission of one or more stages, or their out-of-sequence use, produces an incomplete or inadequate story. Folk tales contain the simplest story grammar. Because folk tales are handed down orally through generations, they are shaped and stylized into a definite grammatical sequence. The individual steps are:

- Setting.   Establishes the overall situation, including the intro-
                       duction of key characters.
- Precipitating   Marks the start of the main story.
  event.
- Action.   Represents the steps taken in response to the precipitating
                       event.
- Response.   Represents the reactions to the steps. In long stories,
                       both the action and the response steps may be repeated
                       several times.
- Resolution.   Marks the end of the story.

Applying Story Grammar
To a Folk Tale

- Setting.   Once upon a time there was a king with two daughters.
                       One princess was beautiful and kind, but the other was
                       jealous and cruel.
- Precipitating   One day the cruel sister gave the kind sister a potion
  event.   that put her to sleep, because the cruel sister wanted to
                       rule the kingdom herself. No one could wake the
                       sleeping princess.
- Action.   Many years later, a handsome prince found the sleeping
                       beauty and kissed her.
- Response.   His love reawakened the sleeping princess and together
                       they drove away the cruel, jealous princess.
- Resolution.   The prince and princess ruled the kingdom in justice
                       and lived happily ever after.

Similar elements apply to fictional literature, although some writers deliberately modify them for dramatic effect. Story grammars are also present in nonfiction prose, but their structure is more varied than in folk tales. Children who are aware of this story structure are better able to comprehend the text. This is particularly true for school textbooks and other content-area material.

Research shows that poor readers are often less aware of story grammar than good readers. If so, learning activities could be developed to help increase awareness of these story elements. At the simplest level, story grammars provide a framework to guide comprehension questioning. Teachers who direct their questions in sequence to each story unit help make students more aware of the underlying structure. At present, however, few comprehension programs make explicit use of story grammar.

The *Story-Maker*, developed by Andee Rubin, is a notable exception. In *Story-Maker*, children read an initial story segment. The computer program then gives them several choices based on the section they have read. Depending on the student's response, the program branches to a different story outcome. Thus, children can invent and read a variety of stories, all based on the same initial setting. *Story-Maker* also permits children to insert their own story elements in the number of possible outcomes (see Fig. 5.2). This dynamic storybook concept differs from others in that individual elements are not interchangeable but accentuate the underlying story grammars described above.

A program called *Textman*, also developed by Rubin, helps increase awareness of story units by adapting the hangman game. Instead of guessing the letters in a word, students guess the sequence of stages in a story. The computer program introduces story segments in random order. The student must rearrange them to tell a coherent story. Every incorrect guess adds another part to the hangman. Rubin reports that students responded positively to this activity and that it made them more aware of story units.

Ginn's *Suspect Sentences* demonstrates a creative method to increase awareness of story structure even in complex passages. This game involves two or more participants. The first player, the forger, reads a professionally written passage, composes a sentence to match the writer's style, and through word processing, secretly inserts it into the passage. The other players, the detectives, read the passage and try to identify the forged sentence.

```
SUSIE LIVED ACROSS THE STREET FROM
SCHOOL.  WHEN SHE GOT HOME ONE DAY, HER
BIKE WAS NOT IN FRONT OF THE HOUSE WHERE
SHE KEPT IT. SUSIE'S PARENTS WERE UPSET
AND CALLED THE POLICE. THE POLICE SAID A
BIKE HAS TO BE MISSING 24 HOURS BEFORE
THEY'LL LOOK FOR IT.




     type s,c,t,g,h,1-9,<-,->
```

```
1 SUSIE WAS SO SAD SHE DECIDED TO LOOK
  FOR THE BIKE HERSELF.  WHEN SHE WAS
  WALKING DOWN AN ALLEY,

2 <MAKE UP YOUR OWN>






     type s,c,t,g,h,1-9,<-,->
```

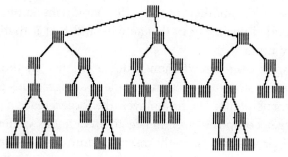

Fig 5.2   An example from *Story-Maker*.

In addition to being an enjoyable game, the process of composing a plausible forgery requires knowledge of correct grammar and spelling and appreciation of paragraph structure. An irrelevant sentence or one written from the wrong perspective is easy to uncover. Similarly, the detectives practice critical reading as they examine each sentence for inconsistencies.

Suspect Sentences also builds into the game significant social contact among the participants. After the detectives have made their selections, the program guides discussion among detectives and forger by asking them questions about their respective choices. These questions make children more aware of the passage structure and help them detect inconsistencies in it.

INTEGRATING THE INFORMATION BASE

Children carry in their heads considerable knowledge about the world in which they live. Psychologists refer to this knowledge base as "schemata" (singular: "schema") or "scripts." A script is a person's condensation of the essential elements of a setting or situation. Games are an example of social settings with very clear schemata. A typical baseball diamond is a well-defined entity in many people's minds, as are the players, umpires, coaches, and spectators. All are interrelated and each conforms to distinct social roles. Children employ these schemata to organize passage information and to infer items missing from the text itself:

> Zoom! The first pitch whizzed past me into the catcher's mitt.
> "Strike two!" shouted the man.
> I looked over to the dugout and knew I couldn't disappoint my teammates. The next swing had to be just right.
> The next pitch came straight down the center. The bat shook as it slammed the ball high into the air.
> Everyone cheered loudly as the ball sailed over the center field fence.

Because most North American readers have well-developed schemata for baseball games, few people have difficulty inferring that "the man" must be the umpire and that the hit is a home run. Similarly, knowledge of the layout of a typical ballpark allows the reader to visualize the action of looking over to the dugout even though this information is not stated in the passage.

Few of the current commercial software make explicit use of a student's schemata in comprehension development. Prior knowledge is either ignored or considered a nuisance to be surmounted when composing comprehension questions. These programs assume that questions that draw on prior knowledge are inadequate measures of reading comprehension because a student's response may be correct as a result of general experience rather than reading comprehension. These questions are described as "passage independent."

An Example of Passage-Independent Questioning

After a passage on snoring, the following question is asked.

3. You can probably guess that snoring happens
   a. only when you are fast asleep.
   b. only when you have a sore throat.
   c. any time your mouth is open for a long time.
   d. any time you are breathing.

Without reading the passage, a student with strong prior knowledge might easily eliminate "b" and "d" as obviously incorrect, and infer that "a" is the most likely answer.

Completely eliminating passage-independent questioning is neither possible nor desirable, because prior knowledge is an integral component of reading comprehension. Passage-independent questions give students the opportunity to compare text to their own internal scripts or schemata. This is especially true for questions involving inference, prediction, or other nonliteral comprehension.

Instead of minimizing the role of schemata in reading comprehension activities, computer programs can guide students in the appropriate integration of prior knowledge with the reading text:

This week, Andrea Clementi's fifth-grade class is reading the poem "Casey at the Bat" by E. L. Thayer. While baseball is a familiar sport to all her students, she wants to use the lesson to demonstrate to her class how prior experience adds structure to a poem.

On the first day, Andrea asks her students to write down as many details as they know about baseball. Each student lists information ranging from the layout of the ballpark to the roles of each player and how points are scored. During the afternoon, a group of students organizes the data and types them in the classroom computer word processor.

On the second day, the class reviews the listing of baseball facts. One student points out missing information about balls and strikes; another complains that the sentences about scoring runs is disorganized. A few editing commands insert the new material and rearrange the scoring rules into a clear structure.

On the third day, the class reads the first part of the poem:

> The outlook wasn't brilliant for the Mudville nine that day;
> The scores stood four to two with but one inning more to play.
> So when Cooney died at second, and Burrows did the same,
> A pallor wreathed the features of the patrons of the game.
> A straggling few got up to go in deep despair. The rest
> Clung to the hope which springs eternal in the human breast;
> They thought, "If only Casey could but get a whack at that—
> We'd put up even money now with Casey at the bat."

As the students read each line of the poem, they transcribe its major points onto their baseball script. Andrea illustrates how the poet's use of selected phrases evokes strong images of the baseball game and the crowd's concern without the need to belabor the reader with extensive description. This initiates a lively discussion on how a writer can take advantage of a reader's background knowledge to shape the tone of a story.

In this vignette the computer serves the indirect role of helping students to express and organize their schemata. While children know many facts about a baseball game, their descriptions often emerge as disjointed strings of details. The word processor's capacity to insert new material and rearrange it quickly helps the class develop a clear basis for understanding the poem.

DEVELOPING MANIPULATIVE SKILLS

The fourth and final key element of reading comprehension is the ability to manipulate the first three components to think flexibly about what is read. This includes recognizing grammatical structure in a passage; relating the information to internal schemata; and remembering, predicting, and evaluating the new information. Which manipulative operations are involved is uncertain, although the most frequently cited ones are:

- Locating.   Using the passage structure to find the desired information.
- Remembering. Recalling the passage information.
- Organizing.   Relating that information to internal schemata.
- Evaluating.   Making judgments about the information.
- Predicting.   Drawing from internal schemata to make reasonable guesses about information not given in the passage.
- Appreciating. Relating personally and emotionally to the information.

Computer Implementations

Drill-and-practice is the most frequently used approach for developing manipulative skills. Students improve their skill at, for example, evaluative thinking by repeated practice in answering questions emphasizing that operation. These curricula often merely indicate whether a student's answer is right or wrong and, as such, the instruction is indirect. Without direct assistance from the curriculum, children must rely on their own ability to infer the appropriate strategies.

Some programs provide more direct assistance by pointing out the key information needed to answer a question. The critical reading comprehension strand of the CCC reading program demonstrates how well-designed feedback helps to guide students toward making correct inferences. When students make an inappropriate response, the computer repeats the information that disproves their answer.

THE TIME OF DAY REFERRED TO IN THIS PASSAGE IS MOST LIKELY _____

A. MORNING
B. MID-DAY
C. EVENING
D. NIGHT

YOUR ANSWER: **C**

THE NARRATOR MENTIONS THAT "IT WAS GETTING LIGHT." THEREFORE, IT COULD NOT HAVE BEEN EVENING.

This type of informative feedback can be more helpful to students than traditional drills that only inform students whether or not their response is correct. In addition to repeating the key information, the program can also highlight relevant information by changing the print color, size, or brightness or by making the words flash on and off.

Reminding students of comprehension strategies is another valuable approach to developing manipulative skills. In the lessons on identifying the main idea of a passage, the *PAL* program developed by Universal Systems for Education first reminds students that the main idea gives all the information in the story, whereas details give only one piece of information. The main idea is usually found by reading the title and by identifying the important items in a story. *PAL* then highlights the key details in a sample passage.

The math problem-solving unit of the *Dolphin* program developed by TSC demonstrates how a difficult comprehension task, such as reading mathematical word problems, can be divided into small steps. In the first step, a student reads the problem and selects the information relevant to solving the problem. When the student selects the correct information, it is highlighted on a screen. If the student selects irrelevant material, tutorial questions guide the student toward the relevant information. In the final steps, which are more distinctly mathematical, students set up the arithmetic expression, compute the correct answer, and apply the computation to a new problem. These problem-solving techniques can be applied to general reading comprehension tasks as well.

Borg-Warner's *Microsystem80: Critical Reading* program adopts a formal approach to developing manipulative skills. This program drills students in the application of the rules of logic, as in the following example:

MR. JONES HAS A WHITE HOUSE OR A GREEN HOUSE. MR. JONES DOES NOT
HAVE A WHITE HOUSE. THEREFORE,

Correct answer: MR. JONES HAS A GREEN HOUSE.

While drills in formal logic appear useful, their value for comprehension
development is questionable. Formal logic problems impose artificial situations that ignore inferences gained from experience. Most students readily
recognize the absurdity in the underlying premise that a house could be
only one of two colors. Logic instruction might be more useful if it were
integrated with prior knowledge.

CONCLUSIONS

Teachers untrained in reading methods often assume that comprehension
instruction is simply a matter of asking many questions about the reading
material. Research studies show that nearly eighty percent of questions
posed by novice teachers involves the recall of specific details explicitly
stated in the reading passage. This narrow approach to comprehension
development ignores the wealth of skills needed to understand a passage.

Excessive emphasis on the ability to recall details is especially unwise
because, as we progress in the computer age, the need for this skill will
lessen. Information banks and the capacity of computers to scan large
quantities of text at extremely rapid rates will enable readers to retrieve
literal information instantly.

On the other hand, readers will need to sharpen their skills for understanding the information presented. Unlike the human mind, computers
are almost totally incapable of inference, drawing conclusions, evaluating
the relevance of material, or applying knowledge to a new problem.
Reading instruction in areas such as comprehension will be much like
instruction in thinking and problem solving.

Consider the example of a history student studying the U.S. Civil War.
Computer data banks can list any wanted fact, ranging from laws enacted,
military tactics, economic data, commercial records, and even the principal

news stories reported in major journals of the day. The history student no longer needs to remember all this information, but now is challenged to discover patterns and to understand the issues encompassing this complex and turbulent period.

Giving Reading a Function

6

Rosalie hates to read. Even though her reading scores are average for a fourth-grader, she avoids reading whenever possible. In class, she finds interruptions that prevent her from finishing her work on time. The room is either too noisy, too hot, or she can't find the needed materials. Her parents take her to the town library and help her select books, but she seldom reads them. Nevertheless, achievement tests show that her reading performance is adequate for her age and grade.

At this point, Rosalie has made good progress toward mastering reading skills, but has yet to incorporate reading into her life as an enjoyable means of learning new information and sharing ideas. As Daniel Fader succinctly titled it, she needs to become "hooked on books." Three things may improve her attitude toward reading:

1. Reading materials that are appropriate for her both in interest and difficulty.
2. Material introduced in a manner that stimulates her interest.
3. Environments in which she uses reading as a functional medium for sharing ideas and information.

All these factors motivate reading by giving it a personal function. They transform reading from an academic activity into a valuable tool used for personal goals.

BOOK SELECTION AIDS

> While Rosalie dislikes reading, she loves animals—especially dogs and horses. A good book for her might build on this interest. Because she prefers fantasy, a fictional account might be better than a book on how to care for animals. Finally, because she is sophisticated for her age, she might prefer books with contents appropriate for young teenagers but written at a fourth-grade level.

Locating books to fit these particulars may be a difficult task. Libraries typically contain several thousand books designated as children's literature. In principle, they have books on all topics, each representing a different perspective, style, and complexity. However, even the most experienced librarian usually becomes familiar with only a fraction of the books available.

The card catalog is the traditional resource for locating specific books. Cards are normally classified by author, title, and general subject matter. However, as libraries have expanded, the card catalog system has become a slow and unwieldy tool. It is particularly cumbersome for locating books that match criteria such as Rosalie's. The book descriptions on each card are too sketchy to provide this information. Time is often wasted flipping through irrelevant cards before finding the most useful ones. So, most people rely on recommendations from friends, teachers, and librarians.

Computers greatly simplify the task of locating books. Computer programs known as *data-base management systems* or *DBMS* search through a large collection of information to locate items that match a set of criteria. A DBMS is specifically designed to solve this type of book selection problem. However, few libraries employ a DBMS as a book selection aid for public use, although the technology is available with minor adaptation. A hypothetical book search might proceed as follows:

READY
SEARCH
YOU MAY SEARCH FOR
  POETRY   FICTION   NONFICTION

   SCIENCE   HISTORY
WHICH ONE DO YOU WANT? **FICTION**
PLEASE ENTER SEARCH TERMS:
1: **TOPIC: ANIMALS**   2124 BOOKS FOUND

ANIMAL IS A VERY BROAD TERM, TRY SOMETHING MORE SPECIFIC.
2: **TOPIC: HORSES**   152 BOOKS FOUND
3: **OR TOPIC: DOGS**   273 BOOKS FOUND
4: **AND INTEREST: GRADE 6**   27 BOOKS FOUND
5: **AND ABILITY: GRADE 4**   6 BOOKS FOUND
6: **END**
DO YOU WANT TO LOOK AT THE BOOK DESCRIPTIONS? **YES**
SELECTION 1

AUTHOR: SHEILA BURNFORD
TITLE: THE INCREDIBLE JOURNEY
PUBLISHER: LITTLE BROWN & CO., 1961.
SUMMARY: DESCRIBES THE ADVENTURES OF A CAT AND TWO DOGS WHO TRAVEL
           ACROSS THE WILDS OF CENTRAL CANADA IN SEARCH OF THEIR
           OWNER WHO HAD LEFT THEM IN THE CARE OF A FRIEND. THE ANIMALS
           WORK TOGETHER TO ESCAPE WILD ANIMALS AND HUNT FOR FOOD.

DO YOU WANT TO SELECT THIS BOOK? **YES**
THIS BOOK IS FILED AS LC NUMBER: PC3503 V6249 I56 IN THE ADOLESCENT SECTION
OF THIS LIBRARY.
THE BOOK IS IN CIRCULATION, DUE BACK 9/15/83
ADDITIONAL COPIES AVAILABLE FROM
  BETHLEHEM LIBRARY, AVAILABLE
  NISKAYUNA LIBRARY, DUE BACK, 9/3/83
  ALBANY CENTRAL HS, DUE BACK, 8/31/83
DO YOU WANT TO SEE ANOTHER BOOK? **NO**

In this hypothetical case, the user selects the appropriate books by specifying search conditions. The computer program responds with the number of books in the collection that fit the set of descriptors. The user can be more specific when too many books are found or broaden the search when too few are available. Once the computer has located a workable number of books, the user can ask it to show a brief description of some of the books. The descriptions are written by educators and librarians, based on their experiences using the book. The descriptions also include information on the local libraries carrying the book and whether the book has already been checked out. The information on availability is easy for the program to obtain because the circulation desk already uses terminals to check books in and out of the library. In situations like these, users do not have to waste time searching for a book that is already in circulation, nor do they need to visit several different libraries to locate a copy of the book.

Data-base management systems have proven to be fast, effective, and convenient tools for organizing information in business and government. For example, data bases permit a user to scan through several thousand United States government publications to locate those on a specific topic. Once the user has selected appropriate search terms, computers can scan through several thousand entries in less than a minute. A comparable manual search through directories and indexes would take several weeks. A book search conducted through a DBMS would not only be fast, but would also locate items that fit a complex set of descriptors, making the search more efficient than is possible with cards.

In a school, children would probably not conduct searches independently. To use the data base effectively, a user must be familiar with its overall structure and the available descriptors. A librarian would conduct the actual searches, although developers of DBMS software are creating systems in which the commands approximate natural conversation. As these systems become established, independent searches by students and parents may be feasible with minimal initial training.

A DBMS search could be ongoing. A reader would enter a list of interests and store them in a central directory. Whenever a new acquisition matched one of these interests, an announcement would automatically be sent to the reader. The interest lists could also be used for news of community events and other advertisements. Librarians could monitor the central directory and channel their new acquisitions toward popular topics.

Data-base management systems such as these have limitations and are only as accurate as the person who enters information into the system. If a librarian misclassifies a book, the mistake may remain unnoticed for a considerable length of time and, as a result, many books may be overlooked. This problem becomes more acute as the size of the data base grows. Most computer-based collections have complex dictionaries of key words to standardize the meaning of each term and thereby minimize misclassification.

The reduction of browsing is a more subtle limitation of data-base management systems. Research studies of shoppers in a supermarket show that about 60 percent of purchases are made on impulse. The purchase may have been triggered by an attractive sale price, by remembering that the item is needed, or by effective merchandising. While libraries are hardly supermarkets, the same phenomenon is present. People find many interesting books in libraries by accident, while searching for a particular book.

A data-base management system is largely ineffective for impulse selections. This limitation may become particularly severe in the totally automated library proposed by some futurists. In this library, a user might browse through a collection using a home computer. When the user chooses a particular book, he or she checks out by computer and receives the book by mail or community courier. Such a system would be convenient for users and would reduce theft and misshelving, but it might backfire and reduce circulation. Without impulse selections, readers may check out fewer books.

READABILITY ESTIMATION

Rosalie often complains that reading is too much work. She prefers books that are easy to read but not "babyish." When she finds a book difficult to read, she quickly loses interest.

Estimating reading difficulty, or "readability," could assure appropriate book selection. Several readability formulas currently exist. The most accurate formulas combine average sentence length with the percentage of rare words. This assumes that stories with long sentences and unusual vocabulary are more difficult to read and comprehend. The Spache formula and the Dale-Chall formula are examples of this approach. In using these, a teacher selects several 100-word sample passages from the book. After counting the number of sentences per 100 words, the teacher checks each word individually against a list of the most common English words. It takes about an hour to establish the readability of a book using either formula.

The Fry Formula and Flesch Count use a faster but less accurate method. These formulas also require the measurement of the average sentence length, but instead of rare words, the teacher calculates the number of syllables per 100 words of text. Presumably, difficult material consists of stories that have long sentences and polysyllabic words. A teacher can check the readability of a book using one of these formulas in about half the time needed for either the Spache or Dale-Chall formula.

Readability estimation programs are available for many computers, especially microcomputers. In the automated version, a teacher types sample passages into the computer, which displays the average readability on a video screen in seconds. More sophisticated programs compute readability by applying several formulas simultaneously. Such programs also may list rare words in the samples.

While useful in principle, readability estimation programs have many weaknesses in theory and ease of use. The illusion that readability is a well-defined construct that can be accurately measured is the largest weakness. At best, readability formulas are crude indices of reading difficulty. Mean sentence length is only an indirect measure of syntactic complexity; after all, it is possible to have short sentences that are difficult to comprehend. Moreover, rhetorical concerns such as cohesion, clarity of style, and number of inferences required, are omitted in readability formulas. Personal variables, such as a student's prior knowledge, cultural background and expectations, purpose for reading, and interests are ignored, even though these exert strong influences on reading comprehension. In general, these formulas are valid only under very limited conditions.

Existing computerized readability software make inefficient use of a computer's capabilities. All current formulas are intended for manual

In a survey of the readability research literature, Bertram Bruce, Andee Rubin, and Kathleen Starr found the following conditions essential for the validity of readability formulas:

1. Material may be read freely without external time constraints.
2. The text is honestly written and not devised simply to satisfy the readability formulas.
3. Higher-level text structures such as cohesion and clarity are irrelevant.
4. The purpose for reading that material is irrelevant.
5. Statistical averages may be legitimately applied to individual cases.
6. The local students share the same cultural, social, and ethnic backgrounds as the general population.[*]

---

[*] B. Bruce, A. Rubin, and K. Starr, *Why readability formulas fail.* Reading Education Report No. 28, Center for the Study of Reading, Bolt Beranek & Newman Inc., 1981.

calculation. They are limited to measures such as sentence length and syllable counts because these are easy for human evaluators to judge quickly. More complex aspects of a passage are ignored because they are too tedious for rapid manual calculation. Yet, the computer's speed and accuracy make feasible much more complex calculations. Researchers are attempting to develop readability measures that take advantage of the computer's capacity to perform complex calculations in a fraction of a second. The work underway at Bell Laboratories on automated measures of paragraph cohesion is a promising step in this direction.

Practical problems also limit the usefulness of readability measurement software. Most programs lack a convenient means for entering text samples. The less sophisticated programs are written in BASIC, which imposes severe limitations. For example, commas must be removed from the text because BASIC misinterprets them. Few programs can distinguish between a period used to end a sentence and a period indicating a decimal point or an abbreviation. Inexpensive programs lack an easy way to correct typing errors, thereby rendering the readability analysis less accurate. Entering the text samples is often more difficult than it appears at first glance. These problems can be avoided with more sophisticated computer programs.

In the future, teachers may not need to type the text into a computer. Oral-reading computers, such as the Kurzweil Reading Machine developed for visually impaired individuals, read books directly. When a book page is placed over a special window, the page's contents are read aloud using computer-generated speech. Recognizing text in a variety of print fonts, styles, and layouts is one of the most difficult problems in designing oral-reading computers. Once text recognition is achieved, the computer program could be modified to calculate readability instead of speaking each word. While reading machines are too expensive for exclusive use as readability measurement tools, this application could supplement their reading-prosthetic role for visually impaired persons.

Despite these limitations, readability formulas help calculate an overall estimate of task difficulty. More importantly, they reduce reliance on graded basal readers by providing teachers with an easy way to judge the suitability of other literature. The formulas work best when balanced by the teacher's intuition regarding student interest, prior knowledge, and passage complexity.

READING AS COMMUNICATION

Rosalie dislikes reading because she sees it as a solitary task. She prefers being with friends and talking about mutual interests. To her, reading is something to do when she is alone.

Reading is communication between a reader and a writer. In the past, the two have normally been separated by time and space, making the conversation unidirectional. The reader has seldom been able to question the writer or to participate in plot development. Computers make possible print parallels to verbal conversation. Computer mail, dialogue programs, interactive adventures, and information networks are examples of printed conversation. In each, the reader participates more directly with the text than is possible using books.

Computer Mail

Computer mail is one of the best examples of reading and writing as an interactive process. Schools traditionally encourage children to write letters.

Written correspondence, however, lacks immediacy. Children may wait two weeks or more for a reply. By then, most have forgotten the contents of their initial letter or, even worse, have lost interest in it. In computer mail, letters are received in seconds, permitting same-day responses. A true print-based conversation becomes feasible as participants exchange several electronic letters in the course of a day.

Computer mail has been available on large business computer systems for many years. An employee composes a memo at any terminal and directs the computer to send it to one or more members of the network. When the recipient is using a terminal, a message flashes on the screen, indicating incoming mail. The recipient may display the mail on the terminal screen and quickly compose a reply. When the recipient is not available at the time of transmission, the message is stored in memory until the next session or is printed for hand delivery. Computers can collapse total transmission time to seconds, even when the parties are thousands of miles apart. The speed of computer mail makes it particularly valuable for companies with offices in several cities or countries.

Computer mail also works well in schools. In a research study investigating the effectiveness of computer-assisted instruction for hearing-impaired students, Richard Rubenstein and Anne Rollins installed a computer mail system as part of a school's educational computer network. They planned the computer mail system as a leisure-time activity for the students. Letter writing was not a topic in the writing curriculum that year, and teachers did not assign it to the students. Instead, letter writing took place independent of teacher monitoring. The school's computer mail service became more popular than any other computer activity. At the beginning of the experiment the teachers described their students as children who hated to write, yet the forty children in the study composed over 1,500 letters in the computer mail's first year of operation!

This experiment also demonstrates that a computer mail network does not have to span great distances to be effective. Commercial transcontinental networks exist, but they charge an expensive fee for every message. A simple network linking classrooms in a community, with connections to the library and other local resources, could prove to be a more practical system. Children have more in common with a friend in a nearby class or building than with a distant stranger.

**Some Examples of Computer Mail Messages
Written by Students
at a School for the Hearing Impaired***

TO: (A TEACHER)

FROM: (A GIRL)

    HI ! I WAS HAPPY TO GET YOUR lETTER . I DON'T UNDERSTAND
WHAT SUCCEEDING MEAN. THE ANSWER TO YOUR QUESTOIN ARE I
WANT TO GOTO THE (NAME) HIGH SCHOOL. AND YES, I LIKE THE
TEACHER UPSTAIRS. I DON'T HAVE A BOYFRIEND. I THINK (NAME) WANT
TO WRITE TO YOU. I THINK SHE WANT TO KNOW YOUR ADDRESS.
(NAME) SAID YOU ARE HANDSOME. I THINK YOU ARE CUTE. PIESE
WRITE TO ME.

LOVE (NAME)

TO: (NAME)

FROM: (NAME)

OH, DOWWWWWNNNN WITH THE LAW! OOOOOHH!! OOOOH!
OH, DOWWWWNNN WITH THE FUZZ!!! OOOOOOOOH OOOOOH!!
OH, GET AWAAAAAAAYYYYY FROM ALL! SO WE'LL ALL BE FREEEEEEEE!
OOOOOOOOOOOOHHHHHHHHH! OOOOOOOOOOOHHHHHHHH! LA LA LA LA!
NO MORE CRIMES!!!!!!! OOOOOOOOOOOOHHHHHHHHHHHHHHHH!!!!!!

AND PRAISE PLEASE. THANK YOU. THANK YOU.

---

* R. Rubenstein and A. Rollins, *Demonstration of use of computer assisted instruction with
handicapped children*, Bolt Beranek & Newman, 1978.

Dialogue Programs

Computers with multiple terminals usually let two users converse directly
by typing messages on their respective terminals. This is similar to computer

---

A Chat with *Eliza*, the Computer Therapist*

MAY I HELP YOU?
 I WANT TO TALK.
WHY DO YOU WANT TO TALK?
 IT MAKES ME FEEL GOOD.
DO YOU HAVE ANY PSYCHOLOGICAL PROBLEMS?
 NO I DO NOT.
WHY NOT?
 I JUST LIKE TO TALK.
YOU DON'T SAY.
 ARE YOU BEING SARCASTIC?
WHY ARE YOU INTERESTED IN WHETHER OR NOT I AM BEING
SARCASTIC?
 I DO NOT LIKE TO BE LAUGHED AT.
WHAT DOES THAT SUGGEST TO YOU?
 I DO NOT LIKE PEOPLE WHO MAKE FUN OF ME.
DOES THAT QUESTION INTEREST YOU?
 NO.
ARE YOU SAYING NO JUST TO BE NEGATIVE?
 NO.
PLEASE DO NOT REPEAT YOURSELF.
 OK.
I SEE.

---

* This conversation is based on the *Eliza* program as implemented in P-LISP by Pegasys Systems.

---

mail, except that messages are transmitted as they are typed. This allows for true dialogue between two or more participants, providing even greater immediacy than computer mail.

When a friend is unavailable, children may converse with the computer itself. Computer programs to simulate human conversation already exist. The most famous of these is *Eliza*, named for Eliza Doolittle of George Bernard Shaw's *Pygmalion*. In *Eliza*, the computer simulates a friendly, nondirective counselor conversing with humans through printed messages.

Although *Eliza* was originally developed as a demonstration of a computer's ability to understand human conversation, it could also be a useful educational tool, creating an environment in which children use reading and writing to communicate.

Eliza also demonstrates the potential of computer interactions that closely approximate human language. Whereas current comprehension programs are dominated by drills and multiple-choice questions, future programs might assess comprehension by conversing with a student about the topic read. Such conversational interaction could help children improve their expressive language skills and their reading comprehension simultaneously.

To children, conversing with friends by computer or conversing with *Eliza* is a novel and enjoyable means of sharing information. These children not only practice reading and writing skills, but also learn how to use computer terminals. Computer-based conversation and message networks are becoming more widespread as the number of computers in homes and small businesses increases.

READING FOR PLEASURE
AND INFORMATION

Literature Samplers

Rosalie might be more eager to read books if her curiosity were aroused first. Plot synopses, introductory films, and book excerpts stimulate interest. Each provides just enough information to spark curiosity without revealing the book's entire contents.

Although literature motivators and samplers are routinely used in reading programs, the current generation of educational software has virtually ignored them. Several commercial programs check comprehension after reading a text, but none stimulate interest in a passage prior to reading it. Indeed, few comprehension programs that display text also introduce the passage or ask prereading questions to help children establish reading goals. Designers of many reading programs seem to assume that children are automatically interested in reading the material presented.

This omission arises partly from the lack of appropriate motivational activities on a computer. Motivation is traditionally a teacher's responsibility. Interactive video could prove helpful by being linked to a simple DBMS. This would allow students to search for a book and immediately watch a brief audiovisual presentation on each book found. However, until substantially more versatile computer displays become available to schools and libraries, no one will know whether literature motivators are appropriate for computer implementation.

Adventure Games and Dynamic Stories

Adventure games are popular computer-based activities that can also serve a valid reading function. Developed and sold as challenging amusement for adult players, these games have evolved from *Dungeons & Dragons*, a game in which participants move through a maze of rooms populated by exotic beasts that can be defeated with magic weapons and potions gathered along the way. Players gain points by collecting gold and jewels.

Such adventure games create an imaginary setting that is highly motivating and very challenging. The room descriptions convey an atmosphere of mystery and suspense, while finding the treasures requires careful attention to all aspects of each room. Even after several hours of play, most beginners will have collected only a few prizes.

Several factors make these games an interesting reading activity. One is the absence of right or wrong answers. The computer's messages are phrased to resemble those of a playmate. Even error messages are friendly and nonthreatening ("I don't know how to . . ."). This style of interaction is particularly important for reluctant readers or children with poor reading ability, many of whom are sensitive about their inadequate skills.

The use of natural English commands is another helpful feature. Because most commercial games recognize between 100 and 300 words, the players have significant freedom of response. In addition, the simple two-word commands make the game accessible even to students with poor writing skills.

When examined as a reading activity, the adventure game concept makes possible a nearly infinite variety of exciting stories from a small set of rooms and commands. This may be particularly useful for children

---

ZORK—A Typical Adventure Game Dialogue*

You are in an open field west of a white house, with a boarded front door.
There is a small mailbox here.
Walk east
The door is boarded and you can't remove the boards.
Walk north
You are facing the north side of a white house. There is no door here and all
the windows are boarded up. To the north, a narrow path winds through the
trees.
Walk east
You are behind the white house. A path leads into the forest to the east. In one
corner of the house there is a small window which is slightly ajar.
Open window
With great effort you open the window far enough to allow entry.
Enter window
You are in the kitchen of the white house. A table seems to have been used
recently for the preparation of food. A passage leads to the west and a dark
staircase can be seen leading upward. A dark chimney leads down and to the
east is a small window which is open. On the table is an elongated brown sack
smelling of hot peppers. A bottle is sitting on the table. The glass bottle
contains a quantity of water.
Take big
I don't know the word 'big'.
Take bag
Taken
Walk west
You are in the living room. There is a door to the east, a wooden door with
strange gothic lettering to the west, which appears to be nailed shut, a trophy
case, and a large oriental rug in the center of the room. A battery-powered
brass lantern is on the trophy case.

---

* Reprinted with permission from *ZORK: The great underground empire* by Infocom, Inc.

---

who have limited reading and language skills. Teachers often complain
about difficulty in obtaining interesting and varied stories for these children.
Because the plot changes each time the adventure game is played, the
game provides the needed diversity.

Although the basic concept underlying the adventure game shows much promise, commercial games need modification for school use. Adventure games frequently contain gratuitous violence, with emphasis on destroying as many monsters and enemies as possible. A nonviolent adventure might center on gathering supplies for a camping trip. Forgetting key items then leads to complications during the trip itself.

Because nearly all commercial adventure games have been designed for skilled adult players, they have mazes of substantial complexity and do not limit the readability of the narratives. Beginners need simpler mazes, and those with poor reading skills would benefit from educational games with simple narratives and an easy solution. Teachers should select programs capable of storing unfinished games, because children rarely can complete a game in a single class period. With these modifications, the basic adventure-game design could provide a wealth of exciting reading material for children.

Information Networks

As personal computers become more widely used, community information services or networks are emerging as electronic newspapers or bulletin boards. These networks provide a central resource through which participants can get local and national news stories, community announcements, computer mail, and automated commercial services such as banking, shopping, and travel services. National networks such as THE SOURCE are already available. Special-interest and local-organization networks are also emerging.

Users may access these information networks through standard telephone lines using a personal computer or special *Videotex* and *Teletex* terminals. The user's computer or terminal connects to a modem, a special device that converts the computer's signals into electrical signals that are transmitted on telephone lines.

Using a personal computer allows the user to compose long messages to the central host computer in advance and transmit them at high speed. Likewise, the computer program can store a log of the interaction between the user and the host computer for later reading. Information transmission can thus be set at rates too rapid for immediate reading to reduce tele-communication costs to a minimum, allowing the user to read at leisure after the session ends. Information networks designed for use with personal computers seldom display graphics or employ video special effects, however, because of the lack of uniform graphics commands across computer brands.

Videotex and *Teletex* provide a less costly access to the networks than personal computers. Pioneered in Europe, *Videotex* and *Teletex* use a small terminal that connects to a television set and to standard telephone lines. The terminal displays messages from the central network on the home television screen and allows the user to send messages to the main computer (see Fig. 6.1). Most terminals display pictures and graphics in addition to text. Unlike most personal computer networks, these two systems employ efficient communication codes that permit rapid drawing of complex color pictures.

The principal reading benefit accruing from these information networks is the wealth of high-interest reading material they contain. Reluctant readers who might not be interested in traditional literary forms can access news of community events, messages from friends, recipes, and even adventure games. A user can also request the weather report, sports news, local restaurant ratings, a listing of current movies with reviewers' summaries, or other topics of interest. Accessing these networks would be analogous to reading a newspaper that has the interactive capacity of a video game and, as such, may encourage reading as a normal, everyday activity and thereby stimulate reading skill development.

Information networks can, however, increase a family's expenses substantially. A *Teletex* terminal currently costs about two hundred dollars, and the user must pay a monthly fee for the network services. Networks such as THE SOURCE charge about $7 per hour of evening use and substantially more for daytime use. When network conversation is a daily activity, a person could easily accumulate as much as $100 per month in fees. Telephone charges also increase as the telephone is used for both voice and computer communication.

These costs have important social and educational implications. If networks are to become practical community resources, all residents, not just the wealthiest, must have access to them. A new class of disadvantaged individuals, those without access to the information banks, may soon emerge. These are most likely to be the same people who already have reading deficits. Those who would benefit the most from networks could very well be the last to gain access to them.

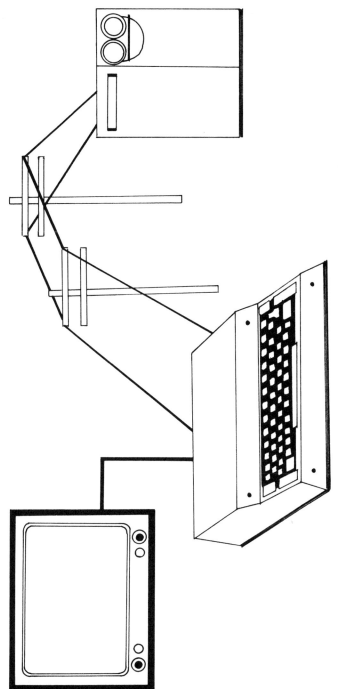

Fig. 6.1   Telecommunications, showing a terminal connected to a host computer via telephone lines.

Differing social perceptions of the importance of information networks in modern life may account for their high cost. People consider resources such as roads and highways as essential services that are supported by taxes rather than user fees. Most individuals would be more reluctant to travel if they were billed monthly for every trip. Future societies may come to regard information resources as equally important as transportation.

Rosalie: Five Years Later

As soon as Rosalie comes home from school, she checks her mailbox— her family's personal computer. To access the community information network, she enters her name and personal identification code and, after a moment, the network displays the messages waiting for her. The first is from the community library: a reminder that a book she has borrowed is due back in three days. This is accompanied by a message that the book on show jumping she requested through inter-library loan has arrived, and an advertisement for a new acquisition on horses—still her favorite subject.

The next message is an invitation from Karen to a birthday party next Saturday. Rosalie types the command "reply" and, automatically, the computer generates the header for a reply to the invitation. She types her response and directs the computer to send it to Karen's network mailbox.

The third is a message sent by her English teacher to all students in the class. It contains clarification of the reading assignment for Wednesday's class—more specific goals for analyzing the next act of a play the class is reading.

Rosalie's last mail message for today is a cryptogram from Greg, a classmate who enjoys sending unusual challenges to his friends. Rosalie stares at it for a moment and mumbles to herself that Greg has devised a really tough one this time. She enters a few commands to save the cryptogram in her personal computer's storage file. She'll work on it later when she is less busy.

Next, Rosalie directs her personal computer to send a report on last night's basketball game to Eric, the editor of the school paper. She typed up the game results early that morning before leaving for school, using a word processing program, and now she wants Eric to approve the article before inserting it in the school newspaper, which is available through the network. In a moment, the item is transferred to Eric's storage space. He will receive it the next time he accesses the network.

Through the information network, reading has become a major part of Rosalie's daily routine in the last few years. Her interest in traditional forms of reading has also flourished, as evidenced by her frequent visits to the library.

Advanced Reading Skills 7

In grade school we learn to read;
After that, we read to learn.

The above generally held misconception is that reading instruction is the domain of elementary schools. By the time youths graduate to junior high school, they are assumed to have totally mastered the skill of reading. Only remedial readers are supposed to need formal reading instruction. For all other students, reading presumably has become a means of acquiring information in other courses and contexts. However, just as skilled workers recognize the importance of well-honed tools, proficient readers continue to develop reading skills—particularly those needed to apply reading to various careers.

Advanced reading skills are less explicitly the domain of the reading teacher. In many schools each academic department assumes responsibility for developing the skills associated with its discipline. In others, such reading instruction takes place in a study skills center that is part of an English or guidance department.

SPEED READING

John is a college-preparatory student at Newport Central High School. He wants to become a doctor or medical researcher, but stories of medical students spending long nights studying assigned texts already worry him. Although John reads well and has consistently received high marks in his courses, he fears his reading may be too slow and labored for advanced studies. He wonders whether speed reading might help him prepare for the demands of medical courses.

John purchases a speed-reading program for his family's home computer after seeing it advertised in a national computer magazine. Each evening, he practices exercises:

LOOK AT THE CROSS

+

After a moment, a word flashes on the screen for an instant. Each time it flashes, its position varies relative to the fixed point.

+   HORSE

This is followed by a multiple-choice test.

WHICH WORD WAS FLASHED?
A.   HOUSE
B.   HOSE
C.   HORSE
D.   HEART

John finds the exercises difficult. At first, he recognizes few of the quickly flashed words. With practice, his performance improves, but he never quite masters the task. Moreover, his reading rate for school assignments does not increase substantially. After a few weeks, he becomes discouraged and practices less regularly. Eventually, the speed-reading disk is relegated to a box of seldom-used programs.

Myths and Misconceptions about Speed Reading

The program John bought is one example of speed-reading gimmicks whose effectiveness is questionable and that are based on grave misconceptions about the psychology of reading. It mimics the elaborate speed-reading devices that existed long before computers arrived in the classroom. These devices include mechanical tachistoscopes that flash individual words, reading pacing machines that move a cursor down a page at a preset speed, and projectors that display text one word at a time.

Myth 1: Speed-reading instruction consists mainly of teaching the eye to see more in a single glance. This myth is based on the introspective impression that fast readers can see a whole line at once and slide their eyes smoothly down a page without stopping to look at individual words. Presumably, the eye can form an accurate image of large sections of text. Readers need only practice using the visual information effectively.

Reading programs like John's result from the theory that reading speed increases when the eye is trained to recognize isolated words more rapidly, particularly those words outside the center of vision, or fovea. In a sense, these programs seek to increase the amount a reader can see in a single glance.

Laboratory experiments have definitively disproved this theory. The eye moves in a series of rapid movements, called saccades, alternating with fixations. It receives information only during a fixation. Indeed, the eye's sensitivity to light is sharply reduced during a saccade. When readers glide their eyes smoothly down a page, the most they see is a gray blur.

During each fixation, the eye sees print clearly only in the foveal region, which extends about eight characters on either side of the point of fixation. Gross features, such as the presence of spaces between words, can be seen up to about 15 characters away. The amount of information obtained from further outside the fixation point is negligible. This limitation is intrinsic to the optics and neuroanatomy of the eye; the eye lacks adequate precision to focus clearly on objects outside the region of foveal vision.

The maximum operating characteristics of the eye, such as the velocity of saccades, the maximum number of saccades per second, and the minimum duration of a fixation are not related to reading ability. These characteristics are unaffected by training; people cannot be taught to move their eyes faster. The eyes make between four and five saccades per second regardless of reading skill. Thus, the eye can neither be trained to see more in a single glance nor taught to move more rapidly.

Span of Perception Research

Computer-controlled displays provide dramatic evidence of the eye's limitations during the reading process. George McConkie and Keith Rayner of Cornell University linked a VDT display with precision eye-movement sensors. The computer program then modified the video display such that only the words in a space around the fixation point appeared clearly, while those outside the fixation point were distorted in a variety of ways. By manipulating the magnitude of the window of undistorted text and the type of distortions used, they could determine how readers use information from outside the foveal region. For example, in the following line of text:

```
Graphology means personality diagnosis from handwriting.
```

If the eye-movement monitor indicated that the reader fixated at the letter "d", the computer displayed the line as:

```
Xxxxxxxxxx xxxxx xxxxonality diagnosis xxxx xxxxxxxxxxx.
```

or

```
Xxxxxxxxxxxxxxxxxxxxxxxonality diagnosis xxxxxxxxxxxxxxxx.
```

or

```
Cnojkaiazp wsorc jsnconality diagnosis tnaw korimnlflrz.
```

In the first example, the spaces between words were kept intact, while in the second, the spaces were removed. In the third example, the overall letter configuration of each word was unchanged but different letters were substituted.

As the reader's eyes move across the video screen, the computer moves the window of undistorted text correspondingly. That is, when the eye's fixation point moves toward the right, the window of undistorted text shifts in the same direction.

Xxxxxxxxxx xxxxx xxxxonality diagnosis xxxx xxxxxxxxxxxx.
Xxxxxxxxxx xxxxx xxxxxxxxxxxxxxiagnosis from hanxxxxxxxx.

The investigators found that readers see a total of about 15 letters clearly, while spaces are seen as far as 15 characters away from the fixation point. Distortions outside this region do not noticeably affect reading speed or comprehension.*

_____

* G. McConkie and K. Rayner, *Identifying the span of the effective stimulus in reading*, Research Report No. 3, Cornell University, 1974.

Myth 2: Eye movements control the reading process. Other programs focus on the theory that proficient readers have smooth left-to-right eye movements across each line, while slow readers' eyes move in an irregular pattern. Perhaps then, slow readers should be helped to develop smooth eye movements, thereby producing a more regular input for the reading process.

Computer programs based on this theory emphasize practice in moving the eyes smoothly from left to right. In a tachistoscopic presentation similar to the program John purchased, a word flashes at the left side of the screen, then at the center of the screen, and finally at the right side.

This approach confuses cause and effect. Smooth eye movements are not the cause of efficient reading, but rather, its result. Regressions and other erratic eye movement patterns indicate that the reader does not understand the passage adequately and must reread sections. The erratic eye movements of poor readers largely disappear when they read material appropriate to their skills. In reality, eye movements are very efficiently controlled by the brain. Except for motor handicaps such as cerebral palsy, people seldom have difficulty controlling their eye movements.

Myth 3: Reading is primarily word recognition. Many speed-reading programs are based on the assumption that limitations to rapid reading rates lie mainly in slow word-attack skills. If only students could learn to recognize isolated words rapidly, they would read faster and with higher comprehension. John's program challenges him to recognize visually similar words presented individually.

Efficient readers do not need to recognize every word in order to read. Research findings show that readers make about five fixations per second and see clearly only about 15 letters per fixation. This means people have an upper limit on reading at less than 1,000 words per minute. To get a faster rate, the reader cannot look at every word. Sentence and story context must fill in predictable words in the text.

Alternative Approaches to Speed Reading

After stripping away the elaborate audiovisual devices and the misconceptions about eye training, two important aspects of speed reading remain. The first is developing the self-confidence to escape from subvocalized oral reading. When children first learn to read, they practice oral reading because it builds on a child's experience with oral language and gives adults an easy way to monitor performance. Many people never break the oral reading habit; they pronounce each word to themselves as they read. In many situations, subvocalized reading is an acceptable strategy. Most readers revert to it when they need to read difficult material very carefully. However, subvocalized speech limits the rate of silent reading to that of speech, or a maximum speed of about 300 words per minute. More rapid rates require the reader to abandon the practice of pronouncing each word.

Tachistoscope programs like the one John purchased provide some incentive to move beyond sounding out each word, but their effectiveness is marred by the presentation of single words in isolation. Although the word appears briefly, a student has unlimited time to sound out the word before making a response, thereby continuing old habits. The incentive to recognize words more rapidly comes only from the psychological pressure of a rapid presentation that demands a rapid response. Few programs penalize the student for stopping to think about the word flashed on the screen.

Programs that present long segments of text encourage students to abandon subvocalized reading because they can display prose too rapidly for speech. The *Comprehension Power Program* developed by I/CT for Milliken Publishing Company is an example. It presents a long story one line at a time. Because the computer can display the lines at a rate from 50 to 650 words per minute, the user can set the program at presentation rates too rapid for pronunciation of every word.

Comprehension questions follow each passage to check reader recall. The developer's decision to superimpose each line of text at the same screen position is, however, a drawback of the Milliken program. Visual perception research has conclusively demonstrated that when two stimuli appear sequentially at the same position, they interfere with the brain's ability to recognize each of them. Milliken's practice of superimposing lines actually makes the effective presentation speed much faster than the nominal maximum rate of 650 words per minute. A more natural presentation might adopt a layout comparable to a normal page of text.

The second important aspect of speed reading involves training the student to be aware of the redundancies in text. Skilled readers do not need to attend equally to all words in a passage. Grammar, both at the sentence and story level, makes many of the words in the text unnecessary for comprehension. Most of the research reports that John will read in medical journals follow a predictable format. An abstract provides an overview of the key points of the study; John should read it carefully to organize the information contained in the paper. The introduction describes the background of the stated hypotheses tested in the experiment. The research methods and specific findings of the study are then presented in detail. Unless John is particularly interested in the research techniques, he may skim these sections rapidly. Finally, the discussion section may require closer attention because it presents the important implications of the study's findings. Awareness of this internal structure will enable John to direct his attention accordingly. Flexible reading makes possible high reading rates without substantial loss in comprehension.

To date, few reading software explicitly draw a student's attention to these reading strategies, even though such software are feasible. Either interactive video or one of the new VDTs, capable of displaying a full 60 lines of text, might be used to take advantage of their capacity to display a realistic textbook page.

A student might be presented with the title of a section and asked to judge the importance of that section to the overall text. If the student decided that it is relatively unimportant, the computer would display that section very rapidly, encouraging the reader to skim the material. If the student judged the section to be very important, the display would advance slowly, allowing more time for careful reading. In this way, the program would encourage a flexible reading strategy whereby the rate varied according to the reader's needs. This activity could be made analogous to a road race game. Using a throttle-like control, students could adjust text presentation speed to fit the difficulty and importance of individual text segments. Points would be awarded to readers who complete the course rapidly and with good comprehension.

Well-designed lessons in speed reading enable a student to read more rapidly, but the effectiveness of these lessons does not arise from training the eye to see more in a glance or to move more efficiently. The lessons help the student abandon the habit of pronouncing every word and become more aware of the predictable structure of most text.

While speed reading is a valuable study tool, it is not applicable in all situations. Many readers may prefer to savor the subtleties of poetry or a favorite story by reading slowly. Likewise, when reading a sales contract, people are well advised to read the agreement carefully.

SPECIALIZED READING STRATEGIES

Slow, careful reading is the most commonly used strategy to learn the information in a book chapter or other content-area material. Few students do much more than this, hoping to comprehend the information after a single reading. Many students underline key passages or take notes as well. However, both laboratory research and practical experience show that underlining and note taking add little to comprehension beyond that afforded by careful reading.

Reading a passage only once is inefficient because a reader may have little basis on which to build comprehension until after the passage is completed. The reader must simultaneously infer the overall direction of the passage and judge the relevance of details in the passage. Learning is more efficient when students first form an overview of the important ideas and then read to fill in the details. The SQ3R method is an example of this approach. Although it may appear more cumbersome than just reading the passage once, studies show that it results in more efficient learning. SQ3R divides studying into five steps:

- *Survey.*   Skim the chapter to form an overview of its contents.
- *Question.* Prepare a series of questions based on the major sections of the chapter.

- *Read.* Read the chapter, paying particular attention to those sections that answer the questions.
- *Recite.* After reading the chapter, close the book and try to answer each of the questions prepared earlier.
- *Review.* If unable to answer one of the questions, reread the relevant sections of the chapter to find material that might provide the answer.

Surveying. Surveying efficiently requires reading strategies that identify the important information in a text before reading the whole text. Several strategies have been advocated for locating this information:

1. Read only the titles, section heads, and illustration captions.
2. Read the first sentence of each paragraph; this sentence usually contains the paragraph's main idea.
3. Look for words that are underlined, italicized, bold-faced, or otherwise emphasized in the text.

The capacity of computers to modify text dynamically can help direct the reader's attention to these strategies. For example, a computer program can display text in the following way:*

THE MEANING OF BOOKKEEPING

Why records are important
    The owner or the manager of a modern business is called upon to make many decisions. Xxx xxxxxx xx xxx xxxxxxxx xxxxxxx xxxxxxx xxxx xxx xxxxxxxx xx xxx xxxxx xxxx xxxxx xxx xxxxxxxx xx xxxxx. Xx xx xxxxxxxxx xxxxxxxxx xx xxxx xxxxxxxx xxx xxxxxxx xxxxxxxxx xxxxxxx xx x xxxxx xxx xxxxxxxxx xxxxxxxxxx.
    Federal, state and local laws require businesses to collect and remit various taxes. Xxxx xxxx xxxxxxx xxxxxxxxxx xx xxxxxxxx xxxxxxxx xxxxxxxxxx xxxxxxx xx xxxxx xxxxxxxxxx xxxxxxxx xx xxxxx xxxxx.
What is bookkeeping?
    Bookkeeping is a system of recording financial information for a business, a club, a school system, or any organization. Xx xxx xxxxx xx xxxxxxxxxxx xx xxx xxxxxxxxx xxxxxxxxx xxxx xxxxxxxx xxxxxxx.

---

* The text in this example is excerpted from A. Janis & M. Miller, *Fundamentals of modern bookkeeping.* (New York: Pitman Publishing Co., 1965), p. 3.

This display realistically models reading of selected sections of text and could build efficient skimming strategies. Because the computer does all the work of selecting key passages, however, this activity is inherently passive and should be used only to introduce this reading strategy.

Transforming the survey stage into a treasure hunt would make the lesson more interactive. For example, when a page of text appears on the screen, a student races against time to find all the word treasures as quickly as possible. Using a joystick control, the student moves the cursor to key words or phrases and presses a button to capture them. The game's element of speed would also promote mastery of skimming strategies.

Questioning. Questioning improves reading comprehension by providing clearer reading goals. Specific questions give the reader a more accurate way of monitoring comprehension than the vaguely stated general goal of "wanting to understand the information in the chapter."

Students can use word processing tools to enter and edit their questions. Inspecting a file of questions written by the instructor and by other students might also prove helpful. As computer-based grammatical analysis becomes more commonplace, the computer may be able to assist students in effective questioning.

Read, Recite, Review. Students' questions can be printed on paper to be used as a study aid while reading the chapter. If students prefer to read the chapter on the video screen, the computer can display their questions in a window across the top of the screen, allowing them to refer to the questions as they read. It is less advantageous to computerize these last three stages, however. Long segments of text are easier to read in printed form than on a video screen.

LEARNING TO LOCATE INFORMATION

Mark's twelfth-grade civics teacher has asked him to write a term paper about the community zoning ordinances. Residential zoning laws that have been in effect for many years have been used recently to block commercial development and the construction of low-income housing.

This has made them the center of considerable controversy. Mark's assignment is to present the various groups' points of view in this debate.

Mark begins by consulting the encyclopedia at the school library. He finds a brief two-page history of the evolution of urban zoning, beginning with its origins in nineteenth-century Europe. While interesting, the article provides Mark with little insight on the current controversy. The encyclopedia lists seven references, but these are all rare books, unavailable in the local libraries. Mark also checks his social studies textbook but finds no relevant information.

Recent newspaper and magazine stories might be more useful. Mark can use four methods to locate these news stories. Skimming recent copies of these sources is the most direct approach. However, this is very tedious and inefficient, and Mark could waste many days searching through irrelevant material.

Resources, such as the *New York Times Index* and the *Reader's Guide to Periodical Literature,* are another option. These have subject indexes from the major news sources. Unfortunately, the printed indexes are published several months after the newspapers and magazines appear on the newsstands, and recent issues of the index may be unavailable because of library bindery delays. Furthermore, the information contained in these references is printed in a condensed format that Mark might find confusing. For example, the 1982 *New York Times Index* contains no direct references to zoning stories but gives 52 cross-references to related entries. The information Mark needs is scattered throughout the index. While extensive cross-referencing reduces the physical size of the index, it complicates locating appropriate stories. It could take Mark several hours to find the desired information.

Data-base inquiry systems are a significantly more powerful tool. While the contents of these data bases are similar to published indexes, Mark is not confused by cross-referencing because it is carried out automatically by the computer. Because computers search by multiple descriptors, the inquiry systems can locate information at much greater speed than Mark can.

Computer data bases exist for a multitude of topics, from architectural standards to zoological publications. One particularly relevant source for Mark's project might be the *New York Times Information Bank,* available through his library's reference department. This data base contains extracts of all important stories appearing in the major newspapers and news magazines published in North America. Because using this data base requires knowledge of specific commands, a reference librarian helps him to conduct the search.

The librarian starts by asking Mark several questions about the types of stories he wants. What aspects of zoning should be included in the search? What other terms besides zoning might describe the topic? Does he want editorials as well as news? Does he want stories published before a certain date? Does he want international stories?

At first, these questions intimidate Mark, but the librarian's helpful suggestions enable him to specify the type of news items he wants for his project. The librarian types the appropriate commands on her terminal. After a few minutes, she informs Mark that the computer has located 23 articles published in the last two years that relate to his topic. Summaries of the stories will be printed by the information bank and mailed to the library. In four days, he can pick up his printout at the reference desk.

Mark finds the speed of this search a bit too magical and would like to conduct his own search. His friend Andrew suggests that he experiment with a network called THE SOURCE™ services. Andy's parents subscribe to this service, accessing it through their home computer.

The next evening, Mark visits Andy's house. They dial a local number and, after entering a few commands, gain access to the communication network:*

THE SOURCE MAIN MENU

1 NEWS AND REFERENCE RESOURCES
2 BUSINESS/FINANCIAL MARKETS
3 CATALOGUE SHOPPING
4 HOME AND LEISURE
5 EDUCATION AND CAREER
6 MAIL AND COMMUNICATIONS
7 CREATING AND COMPUTING
8 SOURCE*PLUS

ENTER ITEM NUMBER OR HELP 1

NEWS & REFERENCE RESOURCES

1 NEWS AND SPORTS
2 TRAVEL AND DINING
3 GOVERNMENT AND POLITICS
4 CONSUMER INFORMATION
5 SCIENCE AND TECHNOLOGY
6 BYLINES NEWS FEATURES

ENTER ITEM NUMBER OR HELP 1

NEWS AND SPORTS

* Reprinted with permission of THE SOURCE. THE SOURCE is a service mark of Source Telecomputing Corporation, a subsidiary of The Reader's Digest Association, Inc.

1 UPI NEWS SERVICE
2 THE EDITORIAL PAGE
3 UPI SPORTS

ENTER ITEM NUMBER OR HELP **1**

KEY WORDS (PRESS RETURN FOR ALL STORIES): **ZONING**

ENTER STARTING & ENDING DATE—OR PRESS RETURN FOR TODAY: **HELP**

ENTER THE EARLIEST AND THE LATEST DATE FROM WHICH TO RETRIEVE
STORIES IN THE FORM MM/DD/YY-MM/DD/YY. LEAVING OFF THE SECOND DATE
IMPLIES SEARCHING THROUGH TODAY. ENTERING JUST A HYPHEN IMPLIES
SEARCHING FROM EARLIEST ENTRY THROUGH TODAY.

ENTER STARTING & ENDING DATE–OR PRESS RETURN FOR TODAY:–

PICK A STARTING STORY NUMBER—FROM 1 (THE EARLIEST) TO 3 (THE LATEST):
3

READ FORWARD IN TIME (RF), READ BACKWARD (RB), SCAN FORWARD (SF) OR
SCAN BACKWARD (SB)? **RB**

1-20-83 10:59 AES

    TRENTON, N.J. (UPI)—THE NEW JERSEY SUPREME COURT TODAY RULED
THAT EVERY MUNICIPALITY MUST PROVIDE A REALISTIC OPPORTUNITY FOR
DECENT HOUSING FOR AT LEAST SOME OF ITS POOR RESIDENTS.
    IN SEVEN UNANIMOUS VOTES, THE STATE'S HIGHEST COURT REAFFIRMED
ITS STAND TAKEN IN 1975 THAT EXCLUSIONARY ZONING TO KEEP OUT THE
POOR WILL NOT BE TOLERATED. . . .

As the news story appears on the screen, Mark exclaims: "That's
today's date! We're reading this story before it appears in the papers."

Information banks are revolutionizing the reference collections of libraries
and transforming people's access to news and reference materials. Whereas
manual searches of a library's holdings might require several days' effort,
computer-based searches can locate items within seconds. Likewise, public
information banks like THE SOURCE provide direct access to national
news services. Many libraries have found it more economical to subscribe
to computer services than to printed indexes; the computer services require
less space, are updated more often, and are fast and efficient.

In the home, the cost of using these information banks can be a
deterrent. Usage fees typically range from five to fifty dollars. When the

services are used frequently, these fees can be a significant expense. On the other hand, some community libraries now use the savings from decreased subscriptions to published indexes to offer these computer searches free or at reduced cost.

Another drawback to computer data bases is the lack of serendipity. While browsing through individual news magazines, Mark might stumble on a seemingly unrelated story that contains useful background information for his project. Unexpected discoveries happen much less frequently with data bases because the computer never displays irrelevant or unspecified entries.

NOTE TAKING

Taking efficient, accurate notes is another important reading-related skill. Good note taking requires a strong sense of organization that anticipates the information that will be required and good comprehension skills to recognize and summarize key information.

A lack of organization leads to unusable notes. Physical disorganization results in notes that are easily misplaced. Many students lack an efficient filing system and have trouble retrieving information. The lack of logical organization produces notes with missing information. For example, in writing his term paper, Mark is expected to provide the full bibliographic citation of all reference materials used. Beginners often fail to record this information as they gather their notes. As a result, they waste time retrieving the materials a second time looking for the correct title, author, or publisher.

Computer filing systems can model good organizational skills. In a filing system, or "data-base management system," Mark might first define a standard form to structure all subsequent information stored in that file. For example, the following file structure might help Mark gather material for his term paper:

SAMPLE DBMS SCREEN FOR TERM PAPER NOTES

AUTHOR: _____

AUTHOR: _____

AUTHOR: _____

TITLE: _____
_____

SOURCE: _____
_____

SUBJECT: _____

SUBJECT: _____

SUBJECT: _____

NOTES: _____
_____
_____
_____
_____
_____
_____
_____
_____
_____
_____
_____
_____
_____
_____
_____
_____
_____
_____
_____
_____
_____
_____
_____
_____
_____
_____
_____
_____
_____
_____

Using a computer to record notes may seem extravagant compared to writing the same information on paper. However, several advantages accompany computer usage.

Unlike printed cards, the file structure of the DBMS can be redefined. Redefining the file helps Mark become aware of organization in note taking. For example, subject descriptors become evident when they serve a direct role in locating the information in the DBMS.

Note-taking errors may diminish as computer-based resources become more widely used. There is no technical reason why the output of a computer search cannot be transferred directly into Mark's filing system. Automatic transfer decreases the likelihood that Mark might copy a citation incorrectly. It would also speed up his search measurably.

Using a DBMS program to rearrange information rapidly allows Mark great versatility. Without it, Mark might sort handwritten notes by topic. But when readings relate to several topics, he must write duplicate cards or cross-reference to avoid losing or misplacing the information. Using a DBMS allows Mark to cross-reference material quickly and efficiently. He can file a news article relating to several topics simultaneously. This cross-referencing provides him with the framework for an efficient search. In preparing the section on the role of zoning in residential segregation, for example, Mark could use the DBMS to retrieve all the notes relating to this topic.

Computer-based filing systems facilitate the transition from reading to writing. Most DBMS programs provide a "report writer" capable of storing the sorted notes in a file suitable for printing or for word processing. Mark could use the report writer to arrange his notes as a sequential narrative. He could then use the word-processing software to restructure the narrative into a cohesive text without retyping the notes by hand. He could later use the DBMS to generate bibliography and index.

The ease with which the data-base entries can be converted into prose may introduce new hazards to writing. Mark might be tempted to compose his term paper as a listing of individual entries with only minimal transitions between them. This could result in a paper that lacks an efficient organization, consistent style, and is devoid of critical evaluation. Plagiarism, whether deliberate or accidental could increase with this approach to writing. When Mark gathers background material by searching a computer information bank, which copies the material automatically into his file, he could easily unintentionally make other writers' insights appear as his original thoughts.

Reading Remediation **8**

About one child in seven experiences substantial difficulty in learning to read. For some, reading problems are part of general learning handicaps such as mental retardation. For others, reading problems are a by-product of inadequate sensory or motor abilities. Other reading problems may be caused by inadequate educational opportunity or ineffective reading instruction. For reading-disabled or learning-disabled students, the cause remains unknown. Their reading growth is slowed despite apparently normal cognitive, sensory, motor, and social development.

Some characteristics of computer-based reading instruction make it particularly valuable for reading remediation, and nearly all the programs presented in the preceding chapters are appropriate for reading-disabled students. Many of the most innovative computer-based reading programs were first developed for and tested with remedial students in the continuing search for more effective methods to alleviate learning problems. The learning needs of remedial students are not fundamentally different from those of any other student. A disability may slow the student's learning rate or impose additional special needs, but the basic goals and characteristics of quality reading instruction remain unchanged.

THREE VIGNETTES ABOUT READING DIFFICULTIES

A Learning-Disabled Adult

Peter is twenty-two and has worked for the past two years as a technician in the computer center of a major university. His supervisor praises his work performance, although co-workers notice that he relies heavily on memory and seldom spends time reading the center's technical documentation. They interpret this as a testimonial to his thorough understanding of the computer's operation, but Peter's secret is that he cannot read the manuals. In the evenings, he tries to memorize their contents by listening carefully to his mother as she reads them to him.

Aware of his serious reading problems and wishing to overcome his handicap, Peter visits the reading clinic of a nearby college once a week after work. Their tests show that he stumbles through literature written for fourth-graders. His frequent word-identification errors block his ability to understand what he is reading. He realizes that this reading disability is an impediment to his professional growth and is frustrated by his continued inability to recognize most printed words.

The discrepancy between Peter's reading deficits and his proficiency in mathematics and other academic skills makes him a dramatic example of a reading-disabled adult. This handicap afflicts as many as 10 percent of the population. Its precise cause remains a mystery, and rapid cures are few.

The lack of instructional materials appropriate for Peter was the first problem confronting the reading clinic. The authors of computer-science texts seldom accommodate readers with severe deficits. Books written at the fourth-grade level are too thin in content for an employed professional like Peter. Therefore, the clinic developed customized materials based on Peter's employment at the computer center.

First they devised word-identification drills based on the technical vocabulary Peter needed. Using PILOT, a computer language designed specifically for computer-assisted instruction, they customized word-identification drills originally written for younger students by changing the vocabulary to words more appropriate to Peter's interests and background. Because the PILOT language includes a powerful lesson editor, this conversion took much less time than might have been required to produce a completely new set of lessons.

Next, they created cue cards containing excerpts from the technical manuals. The cue cards presented key information from the manuals, rewritten to accommodate Peter's limited word-identification skills. With some help from his mother, Peter produced most of these cue cards himself. Because he is computer literate, he had no difficulty using word processors to compose and edit them. The cue cards reduced his need to memorize everything. Checking Peter's cue cards at the start of each tutoring session has led to remedial lessons in spelling and writing in addition to word-identification drills.

Although his reading problems have not been eliminated, Peter has shown considerable improvement after attending the clinic for a year. More importantly, he has developed strategies for applying his limited reading skills to the demands of his profession. He believes that the computer-based reading lessons improved his work performance.

A Fourth-Grade Remedial Reader

Irene, a new student at Van Buren Elementary School, is having difficulty in her reading classes. Although a conscientious student, her reading achievement test scores are below average. Her teacher has asked the remedial reading teacher, Janet Moreau, to identify Irene's reading problems and help her catch up with the rest of her class. Ms. Moreau administers a test battery called an informal reading inventory that contains word lists and reading passages.

Six word lists of increasing difficulty make up the first part of the informal reading inventory. Irene reads the lists quickly and confidently. She begins to falter only when the list contains complicated words not normally taught to fourth graders. Her errors are minor deviations from correct pronunciation of the words.

The second half of the informal reading inventory involves a series of reading passages followed by comprehension questions. Irene's oral reading of the passages is accurate, although she reads them in a flat, uninterested tone. Her responses to the comprehension questions are vague or evasive. "It didn't say," she replies.

Unlike Peter, who cannot identify words, Irene's reading handicap is the inability to comprehend what she reads. Her word-identification skills are accurate, but she is unaccustomed to thinking about the ideas in a text. To her, reading is a word-calling activity comparable to the way others might read a list of random words. In rare instances, cognitive deficits can be the cause of problems like Irene's, but a more common origin is a reading curriculum that overemphasizes word identification and phonics instruction. Because Irene is quite articulate when discussing topics that interest her personally, the second cause seems more likely in her case.

Ms. Moreau's principal objective is to increase Irene's awareness of the meaning relationships in text. Activities in which Irene must rephrase passages in her own words seem like a good starting point. With the help of a friend who is a computer programmer, Ms. Moreau devised a paraphrase activity. At the simplest level, a sentence from a reading passage is displayed on the top half of a video screen:

ONE OF MAN'S BEST FRIENDS IN NORTH AMERICA IS THE BIRD.

Irene must rewrite the sentence across the bottom of the screen, putting it in her own words. Word-processing tools help her to enter and revise the text. Her first attempt is almost a direct copy of the original:

ONE OF OUR BEST FRIENDS IN AMERICA IS THE BIRD.

When she presses the "escape" key to indicate that she has finished composing, the computer highlights the words in her paraphrase that are identical to the original and prompts her to try to be less imitative:

ONE OF OUR **BEST FRIENDS** IN **AMERICA** IS THE **BIRD.**

CAN YOU THINK OF A DIFFERENT WAY OF SAYING THIS?

Irene frowns momentarily as she reconsiders the possible meaning of the sentence, and rephrases hers to:

BIRDS ARE GOOD ANIMALS TO HAVE AROUND.

This time the computer accepts Irene's response without comment and moves to the next sentence in the paragraph. Each time, she is challenged to think of a different way of expressing the same idea. Whenever her sentence retains more than three words of the model sentence, the program prompts her to rephrase it.

When Irene has completed several sentences, Ms. Moreau checks her work. She enters a few commands to display the original paragraph and Irene's paraphrase on the screen. They review each sentence and discuss the accuracy of some rephrasings.

After the first lesson, Irene copies the model less frequently and shows greater skill at rephrasing the ideas in each sentence. Later, as her comprehension skills grow, Ms. Moreau increases the challenge by giving her whole paragraphs to rephrase in one step.

Buoyed by the success of this lesson, Ms. Moreau adapts other reading comprehension activities. Using the *Suspect Sentences* game program described in Chapter 5, she takes the role of the forger, entering sentences that are obviously nonsensical in the paragraph context. Irene is pleased by her own ability to spot such fakes. Gradually, Ms. Moreau increases the subtlety of the forgeries until Irene is forced to examine the ideas in the passage carefully to detect them.

Ms. Moreau then tries an adventure game program that she thinks Irene might enjoy playing. Because each episode of the adventure requires making decisions that influence plot direction, Irene must pay close attention to every detail presented in each passage, looking for the clues that will win her prizes. At first, Irene is frustrated by her inability to make progress; she keeps coming back to the starting point of the game. With Ms. Moreau's guidance, she learns to examine each passage very carefully for clues and to apply critical judgment to each new situation. Whenever she collects a new prize, she proudly announces it to her teacher and friends.

Over the next several weeks, Irene's reading comprehension skills continue to improve. More importantly, she has gained confidence in her ability to think critically about what she reads.

A Hearing-Impaired Boy

David is a six-year-old boy with impaired hearing. As an infant, he appeared normal to his parents until they noticed that he did not recognize or imitate the speech sounds of others. As with most hearing-impaired children, David's inability to hear sounds accurately resulted in severely delayed acquisition of oral language. By the time he was five years old, he understood only a few spoken words. He and his parents communicated through a rudimentary mixture of gestures, manual signs, and speech. While this system is adequate for expressing basic needs, it cannot convey more complex information.

David's parents have enrolled him in a special program for the hearing impaired. To increase his English-language skills as rapidly as possible, David's teacher employs Total Communication, which combines all communication modes—oral training, speechreading, signing, reading, and writing. David has also been fitted with an auditory trainer, a combination hearing aid and radio, tuned to receive signals from a microphone carried by his teacher. The auditory trainer helps David to hear the teacher's voice above background classroom sounds.

Even though David's oral vocabulary is small and he seldom speaks more than one-word phrases, his teacher has decided to introduce him to reading through the *CARIS* program, described in Chapter 3, which uses computer-animated cartoons to teach an initial reading vocabulary. *CARIS* presents a list of nouns on a video screen. David may select a noun by pressing any key when a pointer arrives at the desired word. After David makes a selection, the computer draws a picture of the noun on the screen to introduce its meaning. David may then select a verb from a second list. Once he has chosen both noun and verb, the computer program generates an animated cartoon depicting the meaning of the sentence formed.

The computer is located in the school's reading and language arts center. David's teacher, using a program option, has preselected a subset of six nouns and five verbs for his initial reading vocabulary. An aide, trained in Total Communication methods, accompanies David to the computer. She communicates with him using sign language and the auditory trainer.

David enters the computer alcove and expectantly sits in front of the video screen, waiting for something to happen. The *CARIS* program presents the six nouns, and a pointer that scans among them. David looks at the screen with a puzzled expression, unsure of what is expected of him. The aide pantomimes pressing the keyboard. David imitates her and picks the word "HOUSE", largely by accident. When a picture of a house appears, he turns to his aide with a look of surprise and elation. The aide says the word and signs it to him. When the verb list appears on the screen, David picks the verb "GROWS" (see Fig. 8.1). The cartoon house grows until it fills the screen. David's face glows with bewilderment and delight at this strange and wonderful toy.

As soon as the noun list reappears, David eagerly picks the very first item in the list. He continues to select the first item for the next several cycles. Because his teacher had preset the program to display the word lists in a fixed serial order, David keeps getting "THE DOG RUNS". He has grasped the idea that pressing a key selects words, but has not yet discovered the pointer's role. Like many beginners, he finds the cartoons themselves sufficiently interesting so that the repetition of the same an-imation does not bore him.

Each time David selects a sentence, the aide reads it to him. At the first animation of "THE DOG RUNS", she signs the word "dog" on David's leg. He finds this amusing, turns and signs it on her leg. She laughs and comments, "If I can do it on your leg, I guess you can do it on mine. Fine, no problem." At first, he signs "dog" only after seeing her sign, but after a couple of cycles he begins to anticipate the word, signs it independently, and vocalizes "Duh." He is visibly excited by the computer-generated pictures and pays close attention to the screen and his aide's comments.

After four cycles of the same noun-verb combination, David hesitates for a moment before pressing a key, allowing the pointer enough time to reach a new noun, "HOUSE". It is not clear whether his hesitation was deliberate or a convenient accident. He again picks the first verb, "RUNS", and laughs loudly when the house dashes across the screen. In the next several cycles, he combines different nouns with the same verb, "RUNS". His selections are now deliberate, as he attentively waits until the pointer reaches a new word. He cannot read any of the new nouns, but after each one he carefully imitates his aide's sign for the word. She notices that he is working with much more intensity and enthusiasm than he normally shows in lessons.

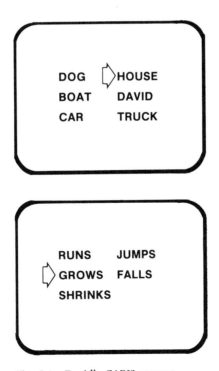

Fig. 8.1   David's *CARIS* screens.

Ten minutes after starting the lesson, David begins to experiment with verbs other than "RUNS". He selects mostly "GROWS" and "SHRINKS"—two actions he is just learning in his language-development lessons. He eagerly imitates the actions of growing and shrinking using exaggerated hand motions. His aide is amazed and says, "Wow, we have a terrible time in class teaching those verbs. It's incredible how quickly he is grasping the action!"

After fifteen minutes of computer interaction, the aide announces that it is time to return to the classroom. David eagerly squeezes out two extra cycles before the aide stops the program. His enthusiasm and curiosity about *CARIS* continue during the day. A week later, his mother reports that he imitates the computer animations using his toys at home.

Over the next several months, David continues to use *CARIS* twice weekly, with no perceptible loss of interest. He quickly learns to recognize the full vocabulary of twelve nouns and thirteen verbs provided in the *CARIS* program. Soon, he graduates to the next level, which introduces typing the selected words. Although his typing is laborious and inaccurate, he is able to locate the majority of letters on the keyboard. The extra effort required to type each word does not diminish his interest.

David's teacher reports that, in his first year at school, he has made considerable progress in all aspects of English-language communication. She believes that the computer activities give him a head start in reading and is looking forward to introducing him to more advanced reading activities in the next school year.

COMPUTERS IN THE
READING CLINIC

Reading problems can arise from a multitude of causes. Irene's problems appear to be the result of a severely imbalanced reading curriculum. David's reading problems are part of a general English-language deficit caused by his deafness. The exact cause of Peter's handicap remains unknown, but some form of neurological dysfunction is possible.

Regardless of the cause, however, the fundamental goals of reading instruction are unchanged. These three students improved their reading skills because mainstream instructional techniques were adapted on computers to accommodate their special needs.

Motivation

Considerable personal effort is usually required of remedial students. As a result, their academic progress is slower than that of their nonhandicapped counterparts. Because they must make the extra effort, they often find it easier to remain passive. David's auditory handicap requires him to focus attention on faint sounds that are nearly unintelligible to him. "Tuning out" is an easy escape. Irene does not expect reading to make sense. It is easier for her to reduce reading to a word-calling game. Peter's repeated failure to master a skill critical to his profession frustrates him. He is often tempted to spend his evenings engaged in more relaxing pastimes than mastering the mysteries of print.

Computers can make reading instruction enjoyable by providing interesting and sometimes amusing visual displays. Passivity diminishes when the rewards become comparable to the personal effort involved. Field observations show that students work longer and more diligently during computer lessons than they do in traditional lessons. David eagerly attends to the *CARIS* program for as long as twenty minutes with no apparent loss of interest. When his turn comes, he immediately starts using the program. As his turn ends, he regularly tries to squeeze out a few more responses before the next student arrives. David exhibits no comparable behavior during noncomputerized lessons.

The popularity of behavior-modification approaches in many remedial classrooms attests to the general awareness of the importance of motivation as a learning factor. Behavior modification uses external reinforcers, often in the form of colorful stickers, special privileges, or candy to reward correct responses. The reinforcers are nearly always unrelated to the skills taught. Many computer-based reading programs directly adapt these behavioral principles and provide pictures and cartoons as visual reinforcers for every correct answer.

While these external reinforcers may be useful, they slow the pace of a lesson and provide no direct support to the skills studied. In some computer-based remediation programs, the frequent use of cartoons and other rewards result in an uncomfortably slow pace. Programs like this waste valuable instructional time, particularly when the reinforcers are irrelevant to reading.

Incorporating reinforcement into the activity itself is a more subtle approach. Instead of being an irrelevant intrusion into the learning task, the reinforcers actually help the student to develop reading skills. The cartoons presented to David are amusing and provide him with information about the meaning of the sentences he composes. Thus, they do not waste the available learning time. Similarly, the combined auditory and visual feedback of the *Talking Typewriter*, introduced in Chapter 3, make it an appealing activity for severely handicapped children.

Endowing the reading activity with a valid personal function is another extension of the intrinsic reinforcement principle. The computer mail system, developed at Bolt Beranek & Newman for hearing-impaired students and discussed in Chapter 6, successfully stimulated student writing because it transformed letter writing into a means for conversing with friends and classmates. In the class that tested the computer mail system, letter writing was never a mandatory activity, nor were prizes given for the best composition. Nevertheless, over 1,500 letters were written in one year! Typing and sending private messages to classmates was, in itself, adequate reinforcement.

Responsiveness

Remedial students need more individual attention than their nonhandicapped classmates. Not only do they need more practice to learn the same reading skills, but they also need a more systematic instructional approach. Irene learned to interpret reading passages by first interpreting individual sentences. She gradually moved to passages that other students interpret without difficulty.

Computer-based lessons gave Irene immediate feedback on her work, reducing the need for constant teacher attention. While Irene worked on her computer-based lesson, Ms. Moreau attended to other remedial students. For David, the computer's responsiveness in displaying words and animations brought a level of intensity to the lesson that otherwise would not have been possible.

Alternative Learning Modes

Remedial teachers have long believed in the existence of preferred learning modalities. They believe that some children are visual learners who acquire reading skills more rapidly through sight experiences, while others are tactile learners who learn better by manipulating objects.

The importance of learning modalities is evident for a sensory-impaired person like David. Without the ability to hear sounds, he knows little about the phonetic structure of speech. To teach him reading through an auditory modality, such as phonics, would be cruel and absurd.

For students like Irene and Peter, whose sensory channels are unimpaired, the role of preferred learning modality is less clear. Despite teacher beliefs, systematic studies of learning rates do not demonstrate any consistent interaction between a child's preferred learning modality and the effectiveness of different reading curricula.

Part of the failure of the modality concept is due to the lack of instructional approaches that truly address the different modalities. Nearly all initial reading curricula assume that a child has a well-developed knowledge of spoken language and introduce reading by building connections to speech. Oral reading, language experience stories, and phonics all seek to develop associations between print and speech.

Reading instruction emphasizing the visual modality has, for the most part, been restricted to flash cards used in a look-say instructional format. Appropriate computer displays make possible approaches to reading instruction that draw more effectively on visual experiences. The cartoons in *CARIS* provide direct visual feedback of sentence meaning, which makes better sense to children who are visual learners.

The visual modality is particularly useful for children who, like David, have inadequate mastery of oral language. His initial reading experiences demonstrate that reading instruction is possible even for children with very poor understanding of oral language. While interacting with the computer program, David learned to read words that were not part of his oral vocabulary. This phenomenon was particularly noticeable with verbs. Educators of the hearing-impaired have noted that teaching verbs to young deaf children is very difficult, because actions are easily confused with the objects that perform the action. Simple computer-generated cartoons enabled David to grasp quickly the distinction between an object and its motion.

Visual displays may even reverse the traditional pattern wherein reading skills always develop after their spoken counterparts. Oral language improvement may accompany newly emerging reading skills in any child.

David spoke more frequently when using the computer than he did during other instructional time. He often repeated the words to himself or commented to his aide about the pictures and actions. Recent longitudinal research on hearing-impaired preschoolers suggests that early instruction in reading may lead to improved speech skills. If this finding is confirmed in future studies, computer-based reading readiness programs may be an effective tool for teaching oral language skills.

Predictability

The mechanistic, repetitive action of a machine is a valuable resource for some children. Predictability is important because many remedial students need repetition for successful learning. Most adults, however, regard repetitious conduct as undesirable. When they encounter a child doing or saying the same thing over and over again, they become impatient, interpret it in negative terms (perseveration), and try to modify the child's behavior. Computer-based reading activities permit unlimited repetition *if* the student so wishes. Field studies of handicapped children engaged in computer-based lessons show that repetition is not always a mechanistic perseveration, but is sometimes a deliberate learning strategy a child uses when attempting to understand a complex system. The following example demonstrates the logic underlying apparently perseverative patterns:

> Tony, an autistic teenager, showed no interest in the *CARIS* animations. After the first animation, he reached to the rear of the computer, turned it off and then on again. This reinitializes the program, causing the computer to ask for the date. He typed:
>
> YDEC71981GHJKFFF.
>
> When the computer asked for the student's name, he typed:
>
> DOITLYPRAYSSSSSSSSSSSSSSSSSSSSSTONY.
>
> Thinking that he might want to type randomly, the teacher stopped the *CARIS* program and set the computer in a mode that displays whatever is typed. He quickly turned the computer off and on again, causing the *CARIS* program to restart. He spent the next several minutes repeating

the program's start-up cycle, experimenting with different forms of the date and with the names of different students in the class. He never confused the date and name requests, although his bizarre spellings prevented him from entering the main program.

During the next month, he used *CARIS* daily under the supervision of his teacher. In one of these sessions, he started the program without a single error or wasted move. He chuckled to himself and glanced at the teacher with a playful, boastful expression. He started the program successfully three times in a row, each time using the name of a different student.

In the next session, he started the program using the name "NUMBERS", having keenly observed the teacher doing so on a previous occasion. This initiates an experimental version of *CARIS* that produces animated cartoons of numbers instead of objects. After using this version for a few minutes, he restarted the program, this time using the name "COLORS". It appeared as if he were deliberately testing the program's versatility, although "COLORS" unfortunately produces no effect in the *CARIS* program.

Flexibility

Predictability in a lesson is important, but the flexibility to modify lessons to fit personal needs is even more valuable. While reading materials should be customized to all students' interests and needs, flexibility is especially important for handicapped readers. Remedial teachers usually accumulate large resource libraries but still need to write their own materials to fit special needs.

Peter's experiences illustrate how a computer's flexibility can increase available instructional resources. Remedial programs for mature, disabled readers have long been hampered by the lack of appropriate materials. This market is too specialized to interest large publishing companies. The few available printed materials are oriented toward teaching English as a second language or teaching culturally-disadvantaged youths.

The capacity of computers to edit or revise existing lessons rapidly, helps address this demand. Their flexibility makes possible customized materials that fit specific interests and needs. Without the help of a computer, Peter's lessons would have progressed more slowly as more time would have been needed to rewrite materials for him.

The *Suspect Sentences* lesson shows how flexible use of a ready-made program can have important educational benefits. By starting with very obvious forgeries, the remedial-reading teacher adjusted the lesson's complexity to accommodate Irene's initial comprehension skill. Unlike items inserted in printed materials that always look "homemade," insertions in computer activities look as professional as the originals.

Fostering Autonomous Control

Behaviorist approaches to reading remediation are based on the assumption that curriculum developers know beforehand the appropriate skills and learning styles befitting each student. Children usually have little or no control in determining any aspect of the learning task. This leads to reading drills that do not match student interests and give the student no sense of personal participation. The problem is especially acute for remedial readers who are often discouraged by their inability to read well.

Computer-based learning can provide microworlds that are within the reach of children. These worlds create a setting in which students can establish their own goals and devise their own activities, as illustrated by the following:

> Sean is an eleven-year-old boy who, according to his teachers, cannot identify any letters. When he enters the computer room for his first visit, he sits at the keyboard and presses the keys randomly. This has no effect because the computer is not yet turned on. Sensing the importance of the moment, the teacher announces the name of each letter pressed. Sean presses letters more rapidly as though testing the teacher. At an unexpected moment he hesitates just before typing, tricking the teacher into saying the letter before he types it.
>
> After a few minutes, the teacher turns on the computer. She introduces Sean to a letter game, written in Logo, that draws a large image of a typed letter on the screen and says its name using a speech synthesizer. At first Sean presses random letters, then he types the alphabet in its correct sequence, followed by his name and the names of objects. He giggles throughout the session.

READING PROSTHESES

Computers can serve as reading prostheses as well as instructional tools. Instead of teaching reading skills, a reading prosthetic translates print into forms accessible to the student.

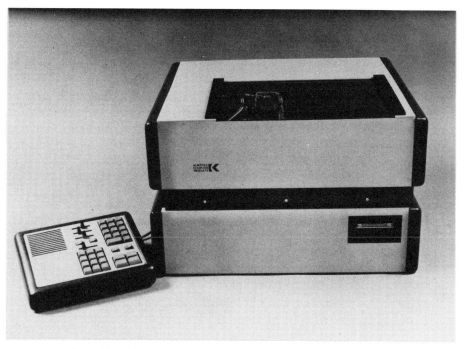

The Kurzweil Reading Machine
Source: Reprinted with permission of Kurzweil Computer Products.

Oral-reading computers, such as the Kurzweil Reading Machine, are the most spectacular of reading prostheses. The Kurzweil Reading Machine looks like an office photocopier and reads aloud any printed material placed against its glass window. It reads accurately most standard print fonts, including that of a good-quality typewriter. It rarely misidentifies words, although the machine's synthetic voice has a distinctly mechanical tone. The user can give commands to reread lines, spell words, or skim material by reading it at speeds faster than normal speech.

Originally developed for blind persons, these machines are useful to anyone who is unable to read print fluently. With a reading machine, a person like Peter would no longer depend on his mother reading technical manuals to him.

Because the current reading machines are too expensive for private ownership, they are found primarily in large public libraries or schools for the visually impaired. As the technology improves, it will be possible to provide personal reading machines to people like Peter. The circuits that recognize printed letters are the most expensive component of reading machines. Inexpensive talking terminals, computers that speak instead of displaying print, are already available.

Magnified print is another valuable reading aid for visually impaired persons who cannot read standard-sized print. More and more people are afflicted with this form of visual impairment as the population of elderly individuals increases. Most printers sold for personal computers can print five characters per inch, or twice the size of standard type. A single computer command changes the printer setting from standard to double-size. This will eliminate the need for special typewriters to prepare correspondence and newsletters for the elderly. Computers can produce these at no extra cost.

CONCLUSIONS

John Eulenberg, a computer scientist who specializes in developing electronic aids for handicapped persons, defines a handicap as "an artifact of society and technology." It is an artifact of society because all people possess limited skills. Some limitations, such as the inability to read, cause social concern, while others, like the inability to sing, do not. As such, the differences between remedial and developmental instruction in reading are quantitative, not qualitative. While remedial readers may require more intense instructional assistance, their basic learning needs are the same.

Reading handicaps are also an artifact of technology. New learning tools provide educators with alternative modes for teaching people with reading and learning difficulties. In the remedial reading center, the responsive quality of computer-based learning systems not only increases student motivation to study reading, but also makes accessible additional learning modalities in a student-centered environment. David's interaction with the computer helped him to learn the meaning of new words and actions.

Reading prostheses are a more radical approach to accommodating the needs of people, like Peter, who cannot read well. Devices such as the

Kurzweil Reading Machine will not teach Peter to read better, but rather will reduce the impact of his handicap by providing an alternative means of accessing the information recorded in print. The professional careers of talented people need not be restricted by their reading difficulties.

*How to Evaluate Software** 9

IDENTIFY THE READING SKILLS INVOLVED

Because of the current wave of interest in computer-based instruction, it is easy to be lured by a reading program with spectacular graphics displays or special sound effects. In the classroom, however, these are secondary to the underlying educational goals of the program. If such software fail to develop skills relevant to reading, they are of limited instructional value.

In general, the manual accompanying most reading programs gives information on the skills emphasized in that product, although the accuracy of this information varies widely. It is wise to check the program personally to assure that those skills are indeed developed and to identify other skills not mentioned in the manual for additional reading benefits. In some cases, a vocabulary program might also teach spelling skills, or a reading comprehension curriculum might include word identification lessons.

Just as general literature adds variety to classroom reading fare, teachers can use software originally designed for home or office applications to develop reading skills. Some computer games are a good source of reading material. Word processing and data-base management programs can be used to teach reading, writing, and study skills.

---

* Additional information on educational software evaluation is given in Chapter 5 of the *Practical Guide to Computers in Education*, the first volume in this series.

CHECK CORRELATION TO OTHER READING ACTIVITIES

Effective reading instruction combines many individual activities in a harmonious pattern. While diversity maintains student interest, the individual parts of a reading curriculum must fit together congruously. Many early computer-based reading programs were designed to operate independently of other classroom activities. Because these programs were used in time-shared settings, they did not anticipate the range of classroom activities likely to occur. Modern software for small computers located in a school building or classroom should be adaptable enough to correlate with other components of the reading curriculum.

Some computer programs provide follow-up activities to be completed at the end of the lesson. In ideal cases, these computerized activities help children apply their new skills to traditional reading forms. In practice, the follow-up materials are often workbook pages that are generally unrelated to the content of the computer-based lessons. More creative extensions could engage students in discussions of the lesson. For example, after a reading activity such as an adventure game, children could discuss or write their strategies in solving the puzzle.

Computer programs in which vocabulary and reading content directly relate to the stories read by students are particularly popular with publishers of basal readers. Good software provide consistency with the original plot, characters, and literary style. Poorly designed software only superficially transpose vocabulary and passage excerpts.

LOOK FOR PROGRAMS THAT EMPHASIZE VARIED CUES

Reading software should accurately model the practice of employing multiple cues in reading. Even when developing a specific skill, such as spelling or phonics, programs should provide additional cues whenever appropriate. For example, well-written word-identification programs present new words in a sentence or story context and may even provide an optional on-line dictionary. The hypothetical word-identification lesson described in Chapter 4 illustrates how these cues can be incorporated into story reading.

FOSTER ACTIVE STUDENT INVOLVEMENT

Children learn best through direct participation in the learning task. Programs that merely require a student to watch the video screen for long periods of time are generally ineffective. An ideal program elicits frequent student interaction.

The quality of student involvement is as important as the quantity. In well-designed programs, students' responses are directly relevant to the skills being taught. Less effective programs present trivial or irrelevant questions. In extreme cases, a child's involvement may be little more than repeatedly pressing the "return" key in an electronic page-turning mode.

PROMOTE SOCIAL AND PERSONAL GROWTH

The popularity of computer-based arcade games and adventure games has led to a plethora of computer activities that are extremely violent and that perpetuate social and sexual stereotypes. In a typical video game, all aliens represent enemies to be destroyed as rapidly as possible. Nonviolent hesitation leads to annihilation and premature termination of the game. In similar fashion, female characters are seldom present in computer games, and if they are, their role is nearly always that of a "damsel in distress," passively awaiting rescue.

Violence and social stereotyping have no legitimate role in educational programs. The hangman game is a typical example of irrelevant violence. In this game, children guess a correct answer before the gallows and victim are completely drawn. The sole instructional purpose for the gallows is to discourage random guessing. Awarding points for the least number of guesses works equally well. Just as interesting books can be written without the inclusion of gratuitous violence and with respect for all members of society, computer-based activities can reflect the same values.

ARE PROGRAM COMPONENTS APPROPRIATE FOR THE INTENDED AUDIENCE?

A well-designed program takes into account the limited skills of young children and avoids overwhelming them with extensive and confusing directions or complex options. Poorly designed software often have operating instructions that are harder to read than the reading material itself. Similarly, reading readiness programs sometimes expect children to type accurately.

Suitability requires consideration of children's preferences and interests. Some special effects that may seem valuable to adults may actually diminish the program's value for children. Robert Yeager found realistic computer-generated pictures of objects to be less intelligible to young readers than simpler stick-figure drawings. At the opposite extreme, some older students may be bored and insulted by cute pictures and reinforcers.

CHECK THE SUITABILITY TO YOUR SCHOOL AND STUDENTS

A program may be carefully designed and well written but still be inappropriate to certain audiences. Some programs employ vocabulary that is specific to one region or culture. Poorly written phonics software may ignore regional differences in the pronunciation of certain words. In other cases, the content of reading selections may be offensive to the values of a local community.

LOOK FOR PROGRAMS THAT ACCOMMODATE A RANGE OF PROFICIENCY

Computer arcade games provide an excellent model for manipulating difficulty. Most games start very easy to give beginners a taste of success and then gradually increase the challenge until they are difficult even for experts. This range of complexity makes a game appealing to players of all levels and encourages participants to try to progress to the next level of proficiency. Few educational programs have adopted this technique.

Programs written for only one skill level are not as desirable as others because a limited range of students can use them. Some children may be overwhelmed by a program's complexity, whereas others may find it quite unchallenging. Better-designed software gradually increase the challenge or permit students to select their own proficiency level before commencing.

LOOK FOR PROGRAMS THAT CAN BE USED BY MORE THAN ONE STUDENT

Activities that permit multiple users serve two important functions simultaneously. First, they increase the availability of a school's limited computer resources. Second, the social interaction that often accompanies group activity is an important learning tool and helps to forge new friendships. Studies show that children prefer computer activities in which they can interact with classmates. Even when playing a video game intended for one player, many children transform it into a group activity by taking turns.

In competitive activities, the presence of additional players permits more complexity than many small computers can handle. For example, programs that check the grammar of student messages are very slow and complex. Allowing the competitors to challenge each other's sentences simplifies the program substantially.

In cooperative activities, each participant can be assigned a different role. For example, in an adventure game one person keeps track of clues while another moves the detective through the maze. By sharing information, players can complete the game more rapidly.

CHECK THE OVERALL PROGRAM DURATION

Classrooms are highly structured environments with time restrictions for every activity. A class period can rarely be extended if a few students have not completed a lesson. Thus, programs must either be sufficiently brief to fit the available class period or provide an option that allows a student to stop the program prematurely and resume the lesson later.

However, the option of storing an unfinished activity can lead to hidden complications. Well-designed software store unfinished lessons under a student's name or personal code, thereby allowing multiple users. But many of the less sophisticated programs do not accommodate multiple users, and the next person who uses the program automatically resumes the previous student's unfinished activity.

LOOK FOR PROGRAMS WITH FLEXIBLE CONTENT AND OPERATION

Considering the high price reading software usually command, it is not cost effective to purchase a program that presents only one or two activities before exhausting its content. A good program provides teachers, and sometimes students, with an editor section for adding or deleting items. The editor extends the usefulness of a program and allows personalization of the contents to the needs of local communities and their students.

When modification options exist, it is important to make certain that the editor is easy to operate. Few educators will bother to struggle through a clumsily written editor. The best designs allow teachers to preview new material before adding it to the activity.

A convenient editor can itself serve a valid instructional role. The saying that the best way to learn something is to try teaching it to someone else holds equally true for computer-based lessons. When teenaged remedial readers are assigned the task of developing additional items for younger students, both groups benefit. The remedial readers review their basic skills in a way that they are less likely to consider childish, while the younger students obtain additional materials for practicing their reading skills.

WATCH THE OVERALL ACTIVITY PACING

Some programs present information at rates too fast or too slow for reading comfort. The fast pace is particularly annoying when the program automatically erases information from the screen. For example, in one program students must read a selection from the manual displayed on the video screen, but if they glance away for a moment, they miss important instructions that are erased automatically.

Some tutorial programs restrict student responses to questions to a brief time period. While this is useful in ideal settings, it ignores the reality that classrooms are subject to many distractions. Interruptions may result in several missed responses. Better-designed tutorials provide some sort of "pause" command that stops the program until the student is ready to respond, unless of course, speed is the prime instructional objective.

Unnecessarily slow-paced programs also exist, although they are less common. Some display words slowly to encourage readers to attend to every word, even though current reading theories suggest that such concentration on every word is unnecessary. In others, the excessive use of extrinsic reinforcers such as cartoons, pictures, and praise messages makes the lesson painfully slow. Well-written software provide the teacher or student with the ability to control presentation rates.

IS THE DOCUMENTATION HELPFUL?

Inadequate documentation is one of the most common shortcomings of computer software—not only in education, but in all domains of computer usage. In many cases, the documentation is sketchy, omitting important information on program features or their application in the classroom. A table of contents, glossary, index, and a one-page summary of key commands are important resources that are often missing from manuals. Well-written manuals employ frequent illustrative examples and sample screens and whenever possible avoid technical terms or define them for novices.

Programs intended for school use ideally should provide two manuals: one for teachers, the other for students. The student edition should be sturdily bound to accommodate rough handling. The teacher's manual should provide suggestions on incorporating the computer activities into the school's general reading program.

Because manuals are easily misplaced, many software developers now incorporate the documentation into the computer program itself. Prefacing the computer lesson with one or more instruction screens is the simplest approach. While helpful for beginners, it forces experienced users to view the instructions every time. Some programs avoid this nuisance by giving users the option to skip the instructions. Presenting the documentation at the start of the lesson poses other problems, however: impatient users may not bother to read the instructions carefully, and novices may forget them once the activity has begun.

On-line help messages are a more convenient and effective way of providing instructions. When in need of assistance, the user presses a key such as "?" or "H" or enters a "help" command. The computer then displays a summary of the key information. For example, in the *Select* word processing program, the commands "H" (help) followed by "I" (insert) display the following screen:

AN EXAMPLE OF ON-LINE HELP

```
PRESS ANY KEY TO RETURN TO DOCUMENT
    COMMAND:         INSERT
    WHAT IT DOES:    ADDS TEXT INTO A DOCUMENT
    HERE'S HOW:      1. MOVE THE CURSOR TO THE PLACE YOU WANT TO INSERT
                        THE TEXT.
                     2. TYPE "I"
                     3. TYPE THE TEXT
                     4. PRESS ESCAPE
```

```
TIPS               - ^ (BOLDFACE), _ (UNDERLINE), [ (SUBSCRIPT),
                     ](SUPERSCRIPT) ARE ON/OFF SWITCHES YOU CAN USE
                     DURING INSERT. DON'T FORGET TO TURN THEM OFF.
                   - BY MOVING THE CURSOR BACKWARDS YOU CAN ERASE
                     THE TEXT TO THE LEFT OF THE CURSOR.
                   - ONLY THE BACKWARDS CURSOR CONTROL WORKS WHILE
                     USING THE INSERT COMMAND.
```

Using screen windows and prompts is another way of providing helpful information. These remind users of their current location in the program and the set of options available to them. In the *Bank Street Writer* shown in Fig. 9.1, text is entered in the center window, while material outside this window informs writers of their current program status, the options

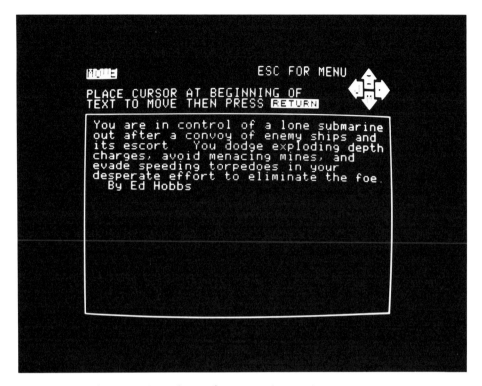

Fig. 9.1 Sample screen from the *Bank Street Writer.*

available, and how to shift to other program modes. This makes the program particularly convenient for novice writers.

EXPERIMENT WITH ALL AVAILABLE OPTIONS

Many programs claim to provide a variety of enhancements that expand on the basic program operation. These might include editors to add reading material, follow-up activities, or management systems that give teachers summaries of student performance. In many cases, these enhancements have been added to the original program as an afterthought and may not be convenient to use. In some cases they may even be inoperable! It is a good idea to test all options, and all combinations of the options, to assure that they fit the school's needs.

TEST A PROGRAM'S ERROR HANDLING BY DELIBERATELY MAKING MISTAKES

The capacity of a program to handle unexpected errors sometimes affords an informal measure of its sophistication. Carefully written programs accommodate all reasonable typing errors without disruption. For example, when a program elicits a multiple-choice response between "A" and "E", typing the letter "G", or pressing the "return" key without making a selection should result in a message similar to the following:

    PLEASE ENTER A, B, C, D, OR E.

Mediocre programs score the impossible selection as an error and proceed with the next step. An unacceptable program might even "crash," that is, cease to operate and need to be restarted. Crash-proof, or bombproof, programs are essential for busy classroom settings.

Deliberately introducing errors can test other types of responses as well. When a program expects a typed word or phrase, the insertion of an occasional minor spelling error, or even an extra space or punctuation mark, should not disrupt program operation. Well-designed programs accommodate such minor mistakes and may either correct the error automatically or respond with a follow-up question as in:

    BACON, HAM, AND VEAL ARE
    MEETS
    DO YOU MEAN MEATS?
    YES

The aforementioned mediocre programs would treat the misspelling as an error just as grave as if the student had entered "vegetables". These poorly written programs discriminate among "MEATS", "Meats", "meats", and "meats.", thereby forcing an unnecessarily strict response accuracy.

CHECK FOR SPECIAL HARDWARE RESTRICTIONS

Computer software are generally not interchangeable among the various brands of hardware, and in some cases, among different models of the same brand because each employs a different recording format. Furthermore, the implementation of many computer languages, like BASIC, is not identical in every machine. Software vendors are usually careful to indicate the brand and model of computer needed for their programs.

Even a specific computer model can have many different accessories. In addition to the basic computer, some programs require multiple disk drives, printers, special input or output devices, memory expansion cards, or programming languages that may not be available at a local school. Most publishers list the required accessories in their catalogs. If this information is missing or unclear, a brief telephone call before ordering can save later disappointment.

Resources

PAPERS RELATING TO COMPUTERS AND READING INSTRUCTION

Allee, J. G., and Williams, R. L. A challenge for the language arts CAI developer. *Creative Computing*, Vol. 6, No. 9 (1980): 122–25.

Anelli, C. M. Computer-assisted instruction and reading achievement of urban third and fourth graders. Ed.D. diss., Rutgers University, 1977. *Xerox microfilms order no.* 78-04582.

Atkinson, R. C.; Fletcher, J. D.; Lindsay, E.; Campbell, T.; and Barr, A. Computer-assisted instruction in initial reading: Individual instruction based on optimization procedures. *Educational Technology*, Vol. 13, No. 9 (1973): 27–37.

Atkinson, R. C., and Fletcher, J. D. Teaching children to read with a computer. *The Reading Teacher* 25 (1972): 319–27.

Atkinson, R. C., and Hansen, D. N. Computer-assisted instruction in initial reading: The Stanford project. *Reading Research Quarterly* 2 (1966): 5–25.

Auten, A. A guide to purchasing a microcomputer. *Journal of Reading* 26 (1982): 268–71.

Barber, B. Creating BYTES of language. *Language Arts* 49 (1982): 472–75.

Bates, M., and Wilson, K. *Iliad: Interactive language instruction assistance for the deaf. Final report.* Cambridge, MA: Bolt Beranek & Newman, 1981. Report no. 4771.

Bergeron, R. D., and Geoffrion, L. D. Computer animation as a tool for teaching reading to the physically handicapped. In M. Cannon (ed.), *Proceedings of the fifth New England bioengineering conference.* New York: Pergamon, 1977.

Blanchard, J. S. Computer-assisted instruction in today's reading classrooms. *Journal of Reading* 23 (1980): 430–34.

Caldwell, R. M., and Rizza, P. J. A computer-based system of reading instruction for adult non-readers. *AEDS Journal* 12 (1979): 155–62.

Coburn, P.; Kelman, P.; Roberts, N.; Snyder, T.; Watt, D.; and Weiner, C. *Practical guide to computers in education.* Reading, MA: Addison-Wesley, 1982.

Dresden Associates. *School microware: A directory of educational software.* Dresden, ME: Dresden Associates, 1980.

Dillingofski, M. S. *Nonprint media and reading: An annotated bibliography.* Newark, DE: International Reading Association, 1979.

Elliott, P., and Videbeck, R. Reading comprehension materials for high school equivalency students on the PLATO IV computer-based education system. *Educational Technology*, Vol. 13, No. 9 (1973): 20–22.

Fletcher, J. D., and Atkinson, R. C. Evaluation of the Stanford CAI program in initial reading. *Journal of Educational Psychology* 63 (1972): 597–602.

Fletcher, J. D., and Suppes, P. Computer-assisted instruction in reading: Grades 4–6. *Educational Technology*, Vol. 12, No. 8 (1972): 42–49.

Frederiksen, J.; Warren, B.; Gillote, H.; and Weaver, P. The name of the game is literacy. *Classroom Computer News*, Vol. 2, No. 5 (1982): 23–27.

Geoffrion, L. D. Computer-based approaches to overcoming language handicap. In J. Megarry, D. Walker, S. Nisbet, and E. Hoyle (eds.), *World Yearbook of Education 1982–83: Computers and education*. London: Kogan Page, 1983.

Geoffrion, L. D. Computer-based exploratory learning systems for handicapped children. *Journal of Educational Technology Systems* 10 (1982): 125–32.

Geoffrion, L. D., and Bergeron, R. D. *Initial reading through animation*. Durham, NH: University of New Hampshire, 1976. ERIC document retrieval number ED 138 929.

Geoffrion, L. D., and Goldenberg, E. P. Computer-based exploratory learning systems for communication handicapped children. *Journal of Special Education* 15 (1981): 325–32.

Goldenberg, E. P. *Special technology for special children: Computers as prostheses to serve communication and autonomy in the education of handicapped children*. Baltimore: University Park Press, 1979.

Golub, L. S. A computer-assisted literacy development program. *Journal of Reading* 17 (1974): 279–84.

Hasselbring, T. S., and Crossland, C. L. Using microcomputers for diagnosing spelling problems in learning-handicapped children. *Educational Technology*, Vol. 21, No. 4 (1981): 37–39.

Hill, J. The Edison Responsive Environment: Its development and use. *Programmed Learning and Educational Technology* 7 (1970): 29–42.

Hines, T. C., and Warren, J. A computerized technique for producing cloze text material. *Educational Technology*, Vol. 18, No. 9 (1978): 56–58.

Kobler, R. The Talking Typewriter and the learning of reading in a disadvantaged community. *Computers and Automation*, Vol. 16, No. 11 (1967): 37–40.

Leviton, H. S., and Thompson, A. K. Person or machine in remedial reading. *Academic Therapy* (1976).

Majer, K. Computer-assisted instruction and reading. *Viewpoints* 48 (1972): 77–98.

Mason, G. E. Computerized reading instruction: A review. *Educational Technology*, Vol. 20, No. 10 (1980): 18–22.

Mason, G. E. The computer in the reading clinic. *The Reading Teacher* 36 (1983): 504–7.

Mason, G. E., and Blanchard, J. S. *Computer applications in reading*. Newark, DE: International Reading Association, 1979.

Mason, G. E., and Blanchard, J. S. Reading teachers put the computer to work. *Classroom Computer News*, Vol. 2, No. 5 (1982): 44–45.

Moe, A. J. Analyzing text with computers. *Educational Technology*, Vol. 20, No. 7 (1980): 29–31.

Moore, O. K. The clarifying environments project. *Educational Technology*, Vol. 11, No. 2 (1971): 73–77.

Moore, O. K. About Talking Typewriters, folk models, and discontinuities: A progress report on twenty years of research, development, and application. *Educational Technology*, Vol. 20, No. 2 (1980): 15–27.

Moore, O. K., and Anderson, A. R. The Responsive Environments project. In R. D. Hess and R. M. Bear (eds.), *Early education: Current theory, research, and action*. Chicago: Aldine, 1968.

Morrison, V. B. Language experience reading with the microcomputer. *The Reading Teacher* 36 (1983): 448–49.

Obertino, P. The PLATO reading project: An overview. *Educational Technology*, Vol. 14, No. 2 (1974): 8–13.

Riskin, J., and Obertino, P. *PLATO early reading curriculum*. Urbana: University of Illinois, 1974. ERIC document retrieval number ED 105 377.

Rubin, A. The computer confronts language arts: Cans and shoulds for education. In A. C. Wilkinson (ed.), *Classroom computers and cognitive science*. New York: Academic Press, 1983.

Serwer, B. L., and Stolurow, L. M. Computer-assisted learning in the language arts. *Elementary English* 47 (1970): 641–50.

Spring, C., and Perry, L. Computer-assisted instruction in word-decoding for educationally-handicapped children. *Journal of Educational Technology Systems* 10 (1982): 149–64.

Steg, D. P., and Schenk, R. Intervention through technology: The "Talking Typewriter" revisited. *Educational Technology* 17 (1977): 45–47.

Tharp, A. L., and Robbins, W. E. Using computers in a natural language mode for elementary education. *International Journal of Man-Machine Studies* 5 (1975): 703–25.

Thompson, B. J. Computers in reading: A review of applications and implications. *Educational Technology*, Vol. 20, No. 8 (1980): 38–41.

Walker, M., and Boillot, M. A computerized reading level analysis. *Educational Technology*, Vol. 19, No. 1 (1979): 47–49.

Weir, S., and Watt, D. LOGO: A computer environment for learning-disabled students. *The Computing Teacher*, Vol. 8, No. 5 (1980): 11–19.

Wells, B. J., and Bell, D. S. A new approach to teaching reading comprehension: Using cloze and computer-assisted instruction. *Educational Technology*, Vol. 20, No. 3 (1980): 49–51.

Wills, M. DOVACK's machines help children read. *American Education* 7 (1971): 3–8.

Wilson, K., and Bates, M. Artificial intelligence in computer-based language instruction. *The Volta Review* 83 (1981): 336–49.

Wisher, R. A. *Improving language skills by computer*. Paper presented at the annual meeting of the Association for the Development of Computer-Based Instructional Systems, Dallas, 1978. ERIC document retrieval no. ED 165 710.

Yeager, R. F. *Using audio with CAI lessons: Experiences of the PLATO early reading project*. Paper presented at the Association for the Development of Computer-Based Instructional Systems, Minneapolis, 1976. ERIC document retrieval no. ED 128 005.

Yeager, R. F. *Lessons learned from the PLATO elementary reading project*. Paper presented at the American Educational Research Association, New York, 1977. ERIC document retrieval no. ED 138 966.

Zacchei, D. The adventures and exploits of the dynamic Storymaker and Textman. *Classroom Computer News*, Vol. 2, No. 5 (1982): 28–30; 76–77.

PUBLIC DOMAIN
PROGRAM LISTINGS

These entries of journal articles include BASIC program listings that can be adapted for most computers.

Baker, A. What's your reading level? *Interface Age*, Vol. 6, No. 5 (1981): 27–29.
Written for Apple II computers, this program uses the Fog readability index. A simple error-correction scheme makes this program easier to use than many others.

Becker, D. A. Flash cards. *Personal Computing*, Vol. 4, No. 4 (1980).
Written for TRS-80 computers, this program displays vocabulary flash cards on a video screen. Although designed for foreign language instruction, it can easily be adapted for practicing new vocabulary.

Carlson, R. Reading level difficulty. *Creative Computing*, Vol. 6, No. 4 (1980): 60–61.
This program uses the Fog readability index. The lack of convenient text entry procedures makes this program less convenient to use than some others.

Derner, R. R. A teacher for your apple. *Personal Computing*, Vol. 4, No. 8 (1980): 48–49.
This program, written for Apple II computers, generates flash cards for a video screen. In the learning mode, a new vocabulary word is displayed followed by its definition. Later, a testing mode displays the new word, accompanied by several definitions. Students must choose the correct alternative.

Fischer, M. Word search. *Personal Computing*, Vol. 4, No. 10 (1980): 34–39.
This program generates word search puzzles for Apple II computers. It prints the puzzle on paper along with a list of the target words and the puzzle's solution. The accompanying article gives considerable information on adapting the program to other computer systems.

Goodman, D., and Schwab, S. Computerized testing for readability. *Creative Computing*, Vol. 6, No. 4 (1980): 46–51.
This readability program, written for WANG 2200 computers, uses the Flesch Count designed for adult materials. The syllabication analysis in this program is more sophisticated than most others. Text input and program operation seem easy and convenient to use.

Hellman, J. M. Library catalog. *Creative Computing*, Vol. 9, No. 3 (1983): 216–55.
Written for Apple II computers, this program catalogs up to 1,000 books. Users may search by author, title, subject, or call number. The program also maintains circulation records for each book.

Isaacson, D. Alphabetize. *Courseware*, Vol. 2, No. 2 (1981): 35–51.
This program displays from three to eight words that children must arrange alphabetically. Bonus points are awarded for rapid responses. A cassette-tape copy of the program is included with the journal.

Isaacson, D. Reading level. *Courseware*, Vol. 2, No. 1 (1981): 11–52.

Text readability is measured using the Bormuth formula. A list of all words appearing in the sample is printed alphabetically, by word length, and by number of syllables per word. A cassette-tape version of the program is included with the journal.

Nicastro, A. R. Extra time: Reading and comprehension tests for language arts. *Creative Computing*, Vol. 5, No. 4 (1979): 62–66.

The program drills students in speed reading by displaying a text in phrase units using a tachistoscopic presentation, followed by comprehension questions. The program is written for DEC PDP-11 computers and permits the insertion of additional stories. It also generates a permanent record of each student's performance.

Noonan, L. Reading level: Determination and evaluation. *Creative Computing*, Vol. 7, No. 3 (1981): 166–73.

This program, written for Commodore PET computers, employs an unidentified readability formula. The method for text input is less convenient to use than others, but the program provides an exact count of the occurrence of various phonic structures.

Nottingham, R. B. Fog index. *Creative Computing*, Vol. 7, No. 4 (1981): 152–54.

This uses the Fog readability index, designed for adult materials. The program is written for TRS-80 computers and is easy to use.

O'Connor, P., and O'Connor, L. Fog index revisited. *Interface Age*, Vol. 7, No. 4 (1982): 22, 148.

Two program listings expand on the original program by A. Baker. One provides an alternative method for estimating the number of syllables in a word, while the other enables application of the Fog index to text previously stored on disk.

Powers, D. E. Perquackey. *Creative Computing*, Vol. 6, No. 4 (1980): 70–78.

This program, written for TRS-80 computers, imitates a commercial spelling game of the same name. Children devise as many different words as possible from a list of ten random letters. The program checks for illegitimate letters, repeated words, or other violations of the rules, and measures the child's speed. However, the program cannot judge the meaning of a letter string.

Rogers, J. F. The first "R". *Creative Computing*, Vol. 6, No. 4 (1980): 62.

This program demonstrates how Radio Shack's speech synthesizer can be used to drill basic sight vocabulary. The program displays a word on a video screen and prompts the student to say it. After a few seconds, the synthesizer pronounces the word and asks the student to repeat it. The program does not endeavour to check the accuracy of the student's pronunciation.

Rugg, T., and Feldman, P. Speed reading made easy . . . via your PET. *Creative Computing*, Vol. 5, No. 1 (1979): 132–33; Vol. 5, No. 3 (1979): 104.

This tachistoscope program flashes brief phrases on a video screen that a student is then required to type.

Schlarb, K. N. Required reading. *Personal Computing*, Vol. 4, No. 12 (1980): 68–71.

Schlarb, K. N. Information source for home and school. *Interface Age*, Vol. 6, No. 2 (1981): 94–95, 138–40.
> The program described in these two articles generates a subject index of classroom books or papers. The program is designed for Apple II computers and enables flexible searching among the entries. The programs listed in the two articles are not identical but operate similarly.

Schuyler, M. R. A readability formula for use on microcomputers. *Journal of Reading* 25 (1982): 560–91.
> This program allows for the use of nine different readability formulas simultaneously. Two are based on a core vocabulary list, while the others are based on syllable counts. The author also validates the formulas by comparing them to an informal reading inventory. The program, designed for Apple II computers, is moderately convenient to use and significantly more sophisticated than other comparable public-domain listings.

Seslar, P. Home librarian. *Personal Computing*, Vol. 4, No. 9 (1980): 30–37.
> This program generates a computer-based index of a small library. Users may search for a book by its author, title, subject, key word, or shelf location.

Smith, R. W. Speed reading with the personal computer. *Creative Computing*, Vol. 7, No. 10 (1981): 162–65.
> This tachistoscope program is written for Atari personal computers. It briefly flashes single words, phrases, or sentences. The sentences are randomly generated from individual parts and are often nonsensical (e.g., "WHEN THE SMART STUDENT WALKED CALMLY UNDER THE TREE SHE MEOWED.").

Webster, J. Searching for Ivan Denisovitch. *Personal Computing*, Vol. 4, No. 7 (1980): 68–69.
> This library catalog program provides an effective procedure for locating books by key words or title. It ignores trivial words and minor punctuation errors.

Whalen, E. A. This Johnny can run the computer. *Personal Computing*, Vol. 4, No. 7 (January, 1980).
> This article contains program listings for three different reading activities. The first presents five words in random sequence and challenges students to alphabetize them. The second requires students to indicate the number of syllables in a word, while the third creates a brief story from randomly selected phrases. All programs are written for Commodore PET computers.

COMMERCIAL SOFTWARE

Wherever feasible, the following summaries of commercial products are based on examination of the actual software. Descriptions that are based solely on a publisher's brochures are indicated by "(P)" at the end of the entry. The listed cost for programs is approximate, because the actual price varies depending on the hardware configuration selected.

This list is by no means exhaustive. New programs emerge nearly every month, and many have undoubtedly escaped attention. Likewise, the inclusion of a program in this list does not indicate an endorsement of the product.

Major Packages

These products comprise several items intended for use by students across a broad range of grade levels. Each seeks to develop multiple reading skills.

TITLE: **COMPUTER MOTIVATED LEARNING LAB**

SOURCE: Random House
201 E. 50th Street
New York, NY 10022
HARDWARE: (not indicated)
COST: $2000
GRADE RANGE: 1–12

Keyed to the *High Intensity Learning Systems* curriculum, this program provides diagnostic testing and instructional programs. Many games supplement skill drills. An on-line management system maintains records on the progress of up to 120 students. (P)

TITLE: **DOLPHIN**

SOURCE: TSC (Time-Share Corporation)
Hanover, NH
HARDWARE: Integrated minicomputer systems; also available: multi-disk systems for Apple II and IBM Personal Computer
COST: (varies according to number of terminals)
GRADE RANGE: 3–8

Dolphin was originally designed as an integrated minicomputer system with computer and software sold as a single unit, but microcomputer versions are now also available. Reading and language arts are divided into very specific subskills (e.g., reading level 3 contains 58 separate skills). Teachers have considerable placement flexibility in assigning students to each skill unit, although students cannot progress to a different skill until the current one is mastered, even if the two are unrelated.

A typical lesson starts with a five-item pretest to check mastery. If the skill is not mastered, the computer automatically branches to a drill lesson. At the end of the lesson, a posttest is administered. If 80% correct, mastery is recorded. If failed, the computer branches to the referral list. This is an optional activity list to which teachers can add items. The default is a message to see the teacher. A message such as "do pages xx–yy in the zz book" can be substituted. Students cannot move to a different skill until the current one is mastered. This program is mentioned on page 95.

TITLE: **LANGUAGE/READING DEVELOPMENT PROGRAM**

SOURCE: Software Technology for Computers
P.O. Box 428
Belmont, MA 02178
HARDWARE: Disks for Apple II or IBM Personal Computer
COST: $175
GRADE RANGE: 3–8

This program provides drill in word recognition, grammar, spelling, and vocabulary. These lessons place greater emphasis than others on rapid response to questions. (P)

TITLE: **MICRO-READ**

SOURCE: American Educational Computer
525 University Ave.
Palo Alto, CA 94301
HARDWARE: Disks for Apple II; also requires Supertalker (digitized speech device)
COST: $1595
GRADE RANGE: 1–8

This program presents drill in phonics, structural analysis, comprehension, and study skills. Each activity employs a similar format: students practice a small series of items until a preset accuracy level (e.g., six correct in a row) is achieved. Mastery is rewarded with simple graphics praise, followed by the next lesson. Speech output is used in the lower levels to present instructions and to support the phonics drills. Lessons run smoothly, although the program's error testing is superficial, particularly at the beginning reading levels. The overall program balance is heavily weighted toward phonics skills.

TITLE: **PAL READING CURRICULUM**

SOURCE: Universal Systems for Education
2120 Academy Circle, Suite E
Colorado Springs, CO 80909
HARDWARE: Disks for Apple II
COST: $100 for required master program disk
$100 for reading package at each grade level
GRADE RANGE: 2–6

Tutorial programs develop phonics, vocabulary, comprehension and study skills. While the programs make little use of graphics and other special effects, each presents the needed reading skills in a sound manner. After a pretest, students who fail to demonstrate skill mastery can study tutorial lessons. Each lesson introduces the skill with generous use of examples. If a student makes frequent mistakes during practice drills, the program reintroduces the skill using simpler phrasing and examples. This program places greater emphasis on explanations and presentation of examples than most others. PAL is mentioned on page 95.

TITLE: **READING CURRICULUM**

SOURCE: CCC (Computer Curriculum Corporation)
Palo Alto, CA
HARDWARE: Integrated minicomputer system, with hardware and software
COST: (varies according to number of terminals)
GRADE RANGE: 3–6

This program is an update of the Stanford CAI project software widely published in reading journals during the late 1960s. Strands are provided for several aspects of reading, including BASIC READING, READING COMPREHENSION, and CRITICAL READING. Each employs a drill-and-practice format to monitor student mastery and to provide practice when deficiencies are found. Teachers can also print individual lessons on paper to use as classroom worksheets. Detailed reports are given for each student.

TITLE: **READING SKILLS COURSEWARE SERIES**

SOURCE: Scott Foresman Electronic Publishing
1900 East Lake Avenue
Chicago, IL 60025
HARDWARE: Cartridges for Texas Instruments Model 99/4A; early levels require speech synthesizer module
COST: $59 per level
GRADE RANGE: 1–6

Two cartridges per grade level are included. Each comes with a thorough teacher's manual that provides the needed instructions, supplementary worksheets, and program management forms. A student reader, keyed to the theme presented in each cartridge, is also provided for the upper levels. Each cartridge includes three or more reading activities built around a common theme. Wherever possible, reading skills are developed in a story structure. The individual activities are brief but make strong use of the computer's color graphics capabilities and are educationally well designed.

REVIEW: *Educational Computer* (September, 1981).

TITLE: **WINDOWS TO READING**

SOURCE: Micro-Ed
Box 24156
Minneapolis, MN 55424
HARDWARE: Disks for Commodore PET
COST: Contents arranged into forty skill groups with cost ranging from $28 to $98 per group

GRADE RANGE: K–3

This program develops basic reading skills with particular emphasis on word identification and phonics. Most lessons are designed to be completed by two students working together—one student as learner and the other as helpful partner already familiar with that skill. (P)

Individual Programs

These programs are more limited in scope and are intended as individual components in a reading curriculum.

TITLE: **ADVENTURES AROUND THE WORLD**

SOURCE: Orange Cherry Media
7 Delano Drive
Bedford Hills, NY 10507
HARDWARE: Disk or tape for Apple II, Atari, or Commodore PET
COST: $67
GRADE RANGE: 3–6
MAJOR SKILLS: Reading comprehension

The program covers four social studies topics with reading passages followed by multiple-choice questions. Periodic graphs accompany pages of text. Comprehension questions consist primarily of factual recall items.

REVIEW: Courseware Report Card (September, 1982).

TITLE: **ADVENTURES OF OSWALD**

SOURCE: Program Design
95 E. Putnam Ave.
Greenwich, CT 06830
HARDWARE: Tape or disk for Atari
COST: $24
GRADE RANGE: K–1
MAJOR SKILLS: Reading readiness
Listening skills

This program is an interactive story for preschoolers. A voice narrates a story about a young boy named Oswald, who falls down a hole and is trapped in a complex maze. By moving a joystick, the child can help Oswald to escape.

REVIEW: Electronic Learning (March, 1983)

TITLE: **ADVERTISING TECHNIQUES**

SOURCE: Micro Power and Light
12820 Hillcrest Rd., Suite 224
Dallas, TX 75230
HARDWARE: Disk for Apple II
COST: $25
GRADE RANGE: 5 and above
MAJOR SKILLS: Critical comprehension

This program teaches children to recognize four major persuasive techniques: Join the Crowd, Decide for Yourself, Remember Me?, and Act Now! (P)

TITLE: **ALPHABETIZING**

SOURCE: Learning Well
200 So. Service Rd.
Roslyn Hts., NY 11577
HARDWARE: Disk for Apple II
COST: $50
GRADE RANGE 2–5
MAJOR SKILLS: Alphabetizing

This game uses a large grid of words arranged randomly. Players rearrange the words into the correct alphabetic sequence. There are four levels of difficulty. (P)

TITLE: **ALPHABET/KEYBOARD**

SOURCE: Random House
201 E. 50th Street
New York, NY 10022
HARDWARE: Tape or disk for TRS-80
COST: $40
GRADE RANGE: K–2
MAJOR SKILLS: Letter matching
Basic typing

Children learn the alphabetic sequence by locating the key that matches a large letter displayed on the video screen. Both uppercase and lowercase letters are drilled. The program does not teach standard hand positions used in typing.

REVIEW: *Educational Technology* (January, 1983).

TITLE: **ALPHABET SEQUENCING AND ALPHABETIZING**

SOURCE: Random House
201 E. 50th Street
New York, NY 10022

HARDWARE: Tape or disk for TRS-80
COST: $60
GRADE RANGE: 3–6
MAJOR SKILLS: Alphabetizing

Students arrange five random-letter strings into proper alphabetic sequence. Practice is given in alphabetizing by first through fourth letters of the strings. The program reinforces successful completion of the lesson with a brief guessing game.

REVIEW: *Educational Technology* (January, 1983).

TITLE: **ANALOGIES**

SOURCE: Micro Power and Light
              12820 Hillcrest Rd., Suite 224
              Dallas, TX 75230
HARDWARE: Disk for Apple II
COST: $35
GRADE RANGE: 9–12
MAJOR SKILLS: Vocabulary

This program drills students in diverse types of word analogy, including synonyms, antonyms, cause/effect, and comparisons. A total of 100 items are provided in the program, along with an editor to add customized lists. A management system keeps records on the scores of up to 200 students. (P)

TITLE: **BOOK CONFERENCE**

SOURCE: Avanti Associates
              9 Marietta Lane
              Mercerville, NJ 08619
HARDWARE: Tape or disk for TRS-80
COST: $19
GRADE RANGE: All
MAJOR SKILLS: Reading comprehension
                  Literary interests

This program is based on the game of "twenty questions." The student tries to guess the title of a famous book by asking questions that can be answered by a yes or no response. Correct guesses are rewarded by a large smiling face on the video screen. The computer's responses, however, are totally unrelated to the student's questions. This program enables correct guesses of nonexistent book titles!

TITLE: **CAUSE AND EFFECT**

SOURCE: Learning Well
              200 So. Service Rd.
              Roslyn Hts., NY 11577

HARDWARE: Disk for Apple II
COST: $50
GRADE RANGE: 2–5
MAJOR SKILLS: Reading comprehension

While embarking on a mountain climbing expedition, players wind in and out of paths leading to the top of the mountain. To reach specially designated spaces, the student must answer cause and effect questions. Incorrect responses cause the climber to tumble back down the mountain. (P)

TITLE: **COMPREHENSION POWER PROGRAM**

SOURCE: Milliken Publishing
1100 Research Blvd.
St. Louis, MO 63132
HARDWARE: Disks for Apple II
COST: $150 per level
GRADE RANGE: 3–8
MAJOR SKILLS: Reading comprehension
Speed reading

The new vocabulary for each passage is first introduced using a sentence context. The reading text is then flashed at a controlled rate one line at a time, followed by comprehension questions. A teacher management system provides detailed analysis of student accuracy for each type of comprehension question. Additional information about this program is given on pages 124–25.

REVIEW: *Electronic Learning* (January, 1982).

TITLE: **COMPU-READ 3.0**

SOURCE: Edu-Ware Services
P.O. Box 22222
Agoura, CA 91301
HARDWARE: Disk for Apple II or Atari
COST: $30
GRADE RANGE: 4–8
MAJOR SKILLS: Speed reading
Word recognition

This program contains four tachistoscopic activities intended for different levels of reading proficiency.

- *Letters:*   After looking at three letters flashed on the video screen, students type them in correct sequence.
- *Words:*   Students type an isolated word flashed on the screen.
- *Synonyms:*   A target word and four word options are flashed. Students select the correct match.
- *Antonyms:*   This has the same format as the synonym activity.

The program operation is smooth but ignores the perceptual limitations of human vision, particularly the synonym and antonym activities that flash the four choices too rapidly for easy reading. Performance is measured using a combination of speed and accuracy. The manual provides detailed information on interpreting speed/accuracy trade-offs.

REVIEW: *Educational Technology* (December, 1982).

TITLE: **COMPU-SPELL**

SOURCE: Edu-Ware Services
P.O. Box 22222
Agoura, CA 91301
HARDWARE: Disk for Apple II
COST: $30 for required system disk
$20 for additional data disks
GRADE RANGE: 4–8, adult
MAJOR SKILLS: Spelling

After reading a spelling word displayed in a sentence context, students type the word from memory. Data disks contain about 1,000 words for each of grade levels 4, 5, 6, 7, 8, and adult. An on-line management system monitors the progress of up to 60 students. (P)

TITLE: **COMPUTER ANIMATED READING INSTRUCTION SYSTEM**

SOURCE: Britannica Computer-Based Learning
425 No. Michigan Avenue
Chicago, IL 60611
HARDWARE: Disk for Apple II
COST: $74
GRADE RANGE: K–1
MAJOR SKILLS: Print awareness
Initial reading vocabulary

This program uses animated cartoons to introduce the reading and spelling of an initial vocabulary. Teachers have considerable flexibility in selecting and labeling pictures and actions. The program is described in Chapters 3 and 8.

TITLE: **COMPUTER DRILL AND INSTRUCTION: PHONICS**

SOURCE: Science Research Associates
1540 Page Mill Rd.
Palo Alto, CA 94303
HARDWARE: Disks for Atari 800;
also requires cassette recorder
COST: $1150
GRADE RANGE: 1–6
MAJOR SKILLS: Phonics

Ten disks drill students in the major phonic elements, from initial consonants to vowel digraphs. A cassette-based sound track provides accurate oral pronunciation of the phonic structures. A workbook supplements the computer-based instruction. (P)

TITLE: **COMPUTERIZED CLASSICS**

SOURCE: Pendulum Press
Saw Mill Rd.
West Haven, CT 06516
HARDWARE: Disks or tapes for Apple II or TRS-80
COST: $25 each
GRADE RANGE: 3–6
MAJOR SKILLS: Reading comprehension
Vocabulary

These programs are extensions of the publisher's *Illustrated Classics* series of comic books based on famous novels. Filmstrips, posters, and other motivational aids are also available. After a child completes one of the books, the computer program poses comprehension and vocabulary questions. Students who make incorrect responses are directed to reread specific pages from the book. This program achieves a better integration of computer media and traditional text than most others.

TITLE: **COMPUTERIZED READING MACHINE**

SOURCE: Southeastern Educational Software
3300 Buckeye Road
Atlanta, GA 30341
HARDWARE: Disk for Apple II
COST: $60
GRADE RANGE: 5–7
MAJOR SKILLS: Reading comprehension
Speed reading

This program contains ten passages and accompanying comprehension questions. Each passage is displayed at a controlled rate, with teacher control of both presentation speed and the amount of text displayed at one time. After the completion of each segment, the program asks comprehension questions, but does not provide feedback on accuracy other than a total score at the end of the lesson. A teacher management section permits assigning specific stories to students, although this component is not as effectively implemented as in other comparable courseware.

TITLE: **CONTEXT CLUES**

SOURCE: Learning Well
200 So. Service Rd.
Roslyn Hts., NY 11577
HARDWARE: Disk for Apple II

COST: $50
GRADE RANGE: 2–5
MAJOR SKILLS: Reading comprehension
                        Vocabulary

This program uses a game format in which players search for hidden treasure along various paths. To stand on special squares, students must define a word from its use in a passage context. (P)

TITLE: **CRITICAL READING**

SOURCE: Borg-Warner Educational Systems
                 600 West University Drive
                 Arlington Heights, IL 60004
HARDWARE: Disks for Apple II
COST: $350 per two levels
GRADE RANGE: 3–6
MAJOR SKILLS: Reading comprehension
                        Logical reasoning

This program uses lessons in formal logic to develop comprehension skills. The range of logical operations includes and/or eliminations, conditional statements, and inductive reasoning. This program is described on pages 95–96.

REVIEW: *Classroom Computer News* (May, 1982).

TITLE: **CROSS CLUES**

SOURCE: Science Research Associates
                 1540 Page Mill Road
                 Palo Alto, CA 94303
HARDWARE: Disk for Apple II or IBM Personal Computer
COST: (not indicated)
GRADE RANGE: 6–adult
MAJOR SKILLS: Spelling
                        Vocabulary

Two students compete to uncover hidden words in an interlocking grid. Fifty different grids are provided. (P)

TITLE: **CROSSWORD MAGIC**

SOURCE: L & S Computerware
                 1589 Fraser Drive
                 Sunnyvale, CA 94086
HARDWARE: Disk for Apple II, or Atari;
                        also requires a printer

COST: $50
GRADE RANGE: 3–adult
MAJOR SKILLS: Spelling
                Vocabulary

This program automatically generates crossword puzzles that can be printed on paper or transferred to a player disk. Players select a location by moving the cursor across the video screen, and can ask for clues and enter answers at any location. They can compare their answers to the completed puzzle or store partly completed puzzles for later use. The program is easy to operate.

REVIEWS: *Courseware Report Card* (September, 1982);
              Infoworld (October 18, 1982);
              Creative Computing (April, 1982);
              Classroom Computer News (March, 1982).

TITLE: **CUSTOMIZED ALPHABET DRILL**

SOURCE: Random House
             201 E. 50th Street
             New York, NY 10022
HARDWARE: Tape or disk for TRS-80
COST: $40
GRADE RANGE: K–3
MAJOR SKILLS: Alphabetic sequence

The program drills alphabetic sequence by asking students to enter the missing letter that completes a sequence (e.g., M,?,O). Graphics and other special effects are not used in the program.

REVIEW: *Educational Technology* (January, 1983).

TITLE: **C-V-C**

SOURCE: Microcomputer Workshops
             103 Puritan Drive
             Port Chester, NY 10573
HARDWARE: Tape for Commodore PET
COST: $20
GRADE RANGE: 1–3
MAJOR SKILLS: Phonics

This program presents seven stair steps on the screen, each containing a blank, a vowel, and a consonant. The student inserts a beginning consonant in each one to form meaningful words. Completing all the steps correctly results in a large happy face followed by additional steps. (P)

TITLE: **DIASCRIPTIVE READING**

SOURCE: Educational Activities
              P.O. Box 392
              Freeport, NY 11520
HARDWARE: Disk or tape for Apple II, Commodore PET, or TRS-80
COST: $245
GRADE RANGE: 3–8
MAJOR SKILLS: Reading comprehension
                    Vocabulary

The program contains both a diagnostic test and practice lessons keyed to the test. The test consists of reading passages followed by comprehension questions. The questions are well-phrased and sample diverse reading skills. The lesson disks provide additional practice at varying levels of proficiency. Drill is the sole instructional mode employed. The exercises are well written but the pace is painfully slow, at one response per 40 seconds!

REVIEW: *Courseware Report Card* (December, 1982).

TITLE: **DO IT YOURSELF SPELLING**

SOURCE: Program Design
              95 E. Putnam Ave.
              Greenwich, CT 06830
HARDWARE: Tape for Atari;
                also requires cassette recorder
COST: $20
GRADE RANGE: 1–adult
MAJOR SKILLS: Spelling

Teachers can create spelling lists for student drill or testing. Students listen to a word on the cassette recorder and enter their spelling into the computer. Students have three chances to spell the word correctly, and are given clues after each try. (P)

REVIEW: *Courseware Report Card* (September, 1982).

TITLE: **DRAWING CONCLUSIONS**

SOURCE: Learning Well
              200 So. Service Rd.
              Roslyn Hts., NY 11577
HARDWARE: Disk for Apple II
COST: $50
GRADE RANGE: 2–5
MAJOR SKILLS: Reading comprehension

This game uses a bingo-like format. Students answer "drawing conclusions" questions and cover a letter when their response is correct. The first person who covers all the letters wins the game. (P)

TITLE: **EARL'S WORD POWER**

SOURCE: George Earl
1302 So. General McMullen
San Antonio, TX 78237
HARDWARE: Disk for Apple II
COST: $30
GRADE RANGE: 4–8
MAJOR SKILLS: Vocabulary
Homonyms

This program teaches several common homonyms. Each is first introduced in individual sentences, with emphasis on their semantic differences. An incorrect homonym selection results in a brief review of the words. After every third lesson, the homonyms are reviewed using stories based on Shakespearean themes.

TITLE: **EARLY WORDS**

SOURCE: Merry Bee Communications
815 Crest Drive
Omaha, NB 68046
HARDWARE: Disk for Apple II
COST: $20
GRADE RANGE: K–1
MAJOR SKILLS: Letter recognition
Word recognition

This disk contains four separate activities, two of which develop reading readiness skills.

- *Early Letters* Presents three letters, of which two are the same letter but in a different type font, orientation, or color. Children must press the number of the box containing the letter that is different.
- *Early Things* Displays three words and three pictures, of which only one word and picture match. Children must type the number of the matching word.

TITLE: **ELEMENTARY LIBRARIES**

SOURCE: Right On Programs
P.O. Box 977
Huntington, NY 11743
HARDWARE: Disk for Apple II
COST: $11
GRADE RANGE: (not indicated)
MAJOR SKILLS: Library selection skills

The disk includes six programs designed to teach children how to use the card catalog, a book's table of contents, index page, and how to locate books on library shelves.

REVIEW: Educational Technology (June, 1982).

TITLE: **FACT OR OPINION**

SOURCE: Learning Well
200 So. Service Rd.
Roslyn Hts., NY 11577
HARDWARE: Disk for Apple II
COST: $50
GRADE RANGE: 2–5
MAJOR SKILLS: Reading comprehension

In this game, players proceed through a shopping mall. On arrival at the entrance to a store, the student must answer a question about the store's advertising claims. (P)

TITLE: **FISHING FOR HOMONYMS**

SOURCE: T.H.E.S.I.S.
P.O. Box 147
Garden City, MI 48135
HARDWARE: Disk for Apple II or Atari
COST: $25
GRADE RANGE: 3–6
MAJOR SKILLS: Vocabulary

This is a computerized version of the "go fish" game in which students compete against the computer to match homonyms. (P)

TITLE: **FLASH SPELL HELICOPTER**

SOURCE: Microcomputer Workshops
103 Puritan Drive
Port Chester, NY 10573
HARDWARE: Tape for Commodore PET
COST: $20
GRADE RANGE: K–12
MAJOR SKILLS: Spelling

A randomly selected word is flashed for 1.5 seconds, after which it must be correctly typed into the computer. Incorrectly spelled words are repeated with an increased display time, while each correct response earns ten seconds of play time on a helicopter video game at the end of the lesson. (P)

TITLE: **FOLLOWING DIRECTIONS**

SOURCE: Learning Well
200 So. Service Rd
Roslyn Hts., NY 11577
HARDWARE: Disk for Apple II

COST: $50
GRADE RANGE: 2–5
MAJOR SKILLS: Reading comprehension

In this game, students travel along a series of paths. At special squares, they must answer questions from a passage that emphasizes giving directions. (P)

TITLE: **FOUR BASIC READING SKILLS**
SOURCE: Brain Box
70 E. 10th St.
New York, NY 10003
HARDWARE: Disk or tape for Apple II or Commodore PET
COST: $60
GRADE RANGE: 5–12
MAJOR SKILLS: Reading comprehension

The program provides drill in four comprehension skills: recalling details, identifying main ideas, drawing conclusions, and sequencing. Most activities consist of a brief reading passage followed by comprehension questions. Student errors are corrected by highlighting the relevant passage sections.

REVIEW: *Educational Technology* (March, 1982).

TITLE: **GETTING THE MAIN IDEA**

SOURCE: Learning Well
200 So. Service Rd.
Roslyn Hts., NY 11577
HARDWARE: Disk for Apple II
COST: $50
GRADE RANGE: 2–5
MAJOR SKILLS: Reading comprehension

This game takes players on a trip around the world. At each city, the student must answer questions based on a passage about that location. (P)

TITLE: **HIDDEN WORDS**

SOURCE: T.H.E.S.I.S
P.O. Box 147
Garden City, MI 48135
HARDWARE: Tape for Atari; also requires a joystick
COST: $17
GRADE RANGE: 1–8
MAJOR SKILLS: Spelling
Word identification

This program generates word search puzzles that students can then solve on-line. Hidden words are selected by using a joystick to move the cursor across the word. There are four levels of complexity, and a time limit further challenges students. (P)

TITLE: **HOMONYMS IN CONTEXT**

SOURCE: Random House
201 E. 50th Street
New York, NY 10022
HARDWARE: Tape or disk for Apple II or TRS-80
COST: $60
GRADE RANGE: 3–12
MAJOR SKILLS: Vocabulary

The program is comprised of six lessons with twenty-five exercises in each. Exercises display a sentence with one word missing, and elicit the correct homonym to complete the sentence. Students gain credit by typing the correct answer in less than 12 seconds. The program does not accommodate minor misspellings. When students have completed a lesson, they are rewarded with a brief arcade-style game.

REVIEW: *Electronic Learning* (May, 1982).

TITLE: **HOW TO READ IN THE CONTENT AREAS**

SOURCE: Educational Activities
P.O. Box 392
Freeport, NY 11520
HARDWARE: Disk for Apple II
COST: $189
GRADE RANGE: 5–6
MAJOR SKILLS: Content-area reading
Reading comprehension

The program contains separate disks for four content areas: science, social studies, literature, and mathematics. The disks are structured identically, with five passages on each disk. The passages themselves are minimally related to the disciplines and the comprehension questions are irrelevant to the content area. The teacher's manual suggests an SQ3R-like format, but this is totally undeveloped in the actual software. Exercise sheets accompany the program.

TITLE: **I DISCOVER PERSONALIZED CHILDREN'S BOOKS**

SOURCE: Creative Concepts
P.O. Box 170
Andover, MA 01810
HARDWARE: Disk for Apple II or Apple III
COST: $395

GRADE RANGE: Readiness
MAJOR SKILLS: Print awareness
                  Interest in books

This is an authoring program to produce personalized books for preschoolers. The books include a child's name, the names of friends, parents, and pets, as well as other comparable information. This program is described on page 49.

REVIEW: *Infoworld* (October 25, 1982).

TITLE: **INDIVIDUAL STUDY CENTER**

SOURCE: TYC Software
               40 Stuyvesant Manor
               Geneseo, NY 14454
HARDWARE: Disk or tape for Apple II or TRS-80
COST: $60
GRADE RANGE: 1–12
MAJOR SKILLS: Spelling
                  Vocabulary
                  Grammar

This program provides several learning games and drills that can be adapted to diverse reading skills. Prewritten lessons teach vocabulary, spelling, and grammar.

TITLE: **INFERENCE**

SOURCE: Learning Well
               200 So. Service Rd.
               Roslyn Hts., NY 11577
HARDWARE: Disk for Apple II
COST: $50
GRADE RANGE: 2–5
MAJOR SKILLS: Reading comprehension

This game takes the student from grammar school through college. Players advance grades by answering inference questions based on student activities at each level. The first person who graduates from college wins the game. (P)

TITLE: **INSTANT ZOO**

SOURCE: Apple Computer, local dealers
HARDWARE: Disk for Apple II
COST: $50
GRADE RANGE: 1–4
MAJOR SKILLS: Word recognition
                  Spelling

Developed by the Children's Television Workshop, this disk contains four separate activities as well as a word list editor that enables adults to customize the contents of the word identification games. The reading-related activities are:

- *Quick Match* Challenges children to respond rapidly if two words are spelled identically.
- *Scramble* Presents a scrambled word whose letters slowly walk down the screen. At each step, they rearrange themselves into a closer approximation of the correct sequence. Children must unscramble the word before the letters reach the bottom of the screen.

Colorful graphics are used throughout the activities.

TITLE: **JABBERTALKY**
SOURCE: Automated Simulations
  P.O. Box 4247
  Mountain View, CA 94040
HARDWARE: Disk for Apple II, or TRS-80
COST: $30
GRADE RANGE: 4–9
MAJOR SKILLS: Language comprehension
  Syntactic skills

This program provides several activities involving the creation and manipulation of random sentences that conform to specific grammatical rules. Available activities are:

- *Free verse* The computer generates random sentences.
- *Alphagrammar* Students guess the letters in a sentence created by computer.
- *Cryptogrammar* Students solve a cryptogram of a computer-generated sentence.
- *Jabbergrammar* Students can edit the word lists and grammatical structures available for the other activities.

The activities are enjoyable and the sentences are often amusing, although students spend much of the time reading sentences created by computer.

REVIEW: *Classroom Computer News* (May, 1982).

TITLE: **KID BITS WORDS FAIR**
SOURCE: Potomac Microresources
  P.O. Box 277
  Riverdale, MD 20737
HARDWARE: Disk for Apple II
COST: $100
GRADE RANGE: K–4
MAJOR SKILLS: Vocabulary
  Grammar

The program provides a very flexible format for language arts drill. Teachers can write lessons for teaching contractions, new vocabulary, grammar, or other language arts skills. Correct student responses add parts to a clown's face. At the end of the lesson, students can view a slide show of the clown faces they have formed.

TITLE: **LETTER RECOGNITION**

SOURCE: Hartley Courseware
P.O. Box 431
Dimondale, MI 48821
HARDWARE: Disk for Apple II;
also requires Cassette Control Device
COST: $27 plus $80 for CCD
GRADE RANGE: K–1
MAJOR SKILLS: Letter recognition
Typing

Children are prompted to type the key that matches a large letter displayed on the video screen. The program can be set to display either uppercase or lowercase letters. (P)

TITLE: **LETTERS AND NUMBERS**

SOURCE: Teaching Tools Microcomputer Services
P.O. Box 50065
Palo Alto, CA 94303
HARDWARE: Tape or disk for Commodore PET
COST: $25
GRADE RANGE: K–2
MAJOR SKILLS: Letter recognition
Alphabetic sequence

The program presents a series of letters or numbers using large characters displayed on the video screen. Students must duplicate the sequence by typing the characters.

REVIEW: *Courseware Report Card* (December, 1982).

TITLE: **LIBRARY SKILLS**

SOURCE: Micro Power and Light
12820 Hillcrest Road, Suite 224
Dallas, TX 75230
HARDWARE: Disk for Apple II
COST: $25
GRADE RANGE: 5 and above
MAJOR SKILLS: Reference skills

This program provides guidance in locating items in a typical library. Units include training in the Dewey Decimal System, the card catalog, and the use of reference materials. (P)

TITLE: **LIMERICK**

SOURCE: Cybernetic Information Systems
P.O. Box 9032
Schenectady, NY 12309

HARDWARE: Tape or disk for TRS-80
COST: $15
GRADE RANGE: (not indicated)
MAJOR SKILLS: Language skills

The program displays or prints limericks created from lists of available parts. Users may augment or change the list contents. (P)

TITLE: **MAGIC SPELLS**

SOURCE: Apple Computer, local dealers
HARDWARE: Disk for Apple II
COST: $45
GRADE RANGE: 2–6
MAJOR SKILLS: Spelling

The program presents a scrambled word that students must retype correctly. It includes eleven lists of frequently misspelled words, and an editor that permits teachers to create additional lists. (P)

REVIEW: *Courseware Report Card* (September, 1982).

TITLE: **MAGIC WAND BOOKS**

SOURCE: Texas Instruments
                Lubbock, TX
HARDWARE: Texas Instruments 99/4A;
                also requires speech synthesizer
                and bar-code reader
COST: Twenty-nine individual titles at $6–$18 each
GRADE RANGE: 1–4
MAJOR SKILLS: Literary appreciation
                Reading for pleasure

This program consists of popular children's literature. Each book page has the usual narrative and a series of bar codes similar to those used on grocery products. The computer reads the text on a page when students slide a special "magic wand" bar-code reader across the lines. This program is described on page 47. (P)

TITLE: **MICRO MOTHER GOOSE**

SOURCE: Software Productions
                2357 Southway Drive
                P.O. Box 21341
                Columbus, OH 43221
HARDWARE: Disk for Apple II;
                also game paddle or joystick
COST: $40

GRADE RANGE: K–3
MAJOR SKILLS: Print awareness

Prereading children can select one of nine popular nursery rhymes. The computer displays a picture based on the rhyme, its lyrics, and plays the melody. Three nonviolent video games for young children are also included. The accompanying manual is particularly useful for novice computer users and has a colorful poster and peel-off pictures of the individual characters. This program is described on page 48.

TITLE: **M-SS-NG L-NKS**

SOURCE: Sunburst Communications, Inc.
　　　　　Pleasantville, NY 10570
　　　　　(commercial licensing under negotiation)
HARDWARE: Disk for Apple II, IBM Personal Computer, or Atari
COST: (prepublication)
GRADE RANGE: 4–8
MAJOR SKILLS: Reading comprehension
　　　　　　　Language skills
　　　　　　　Spelling

The program contains literature excerpts from several famous children's stories. Students can choose any of several deletion patterns such as omitting all vowels, all consonants, the first word of each sentence, etc. Students then read the passage and try to guess the deleted items. The computer program monitors the accuracy of student guesses.

TITLE: **NEWBERRY WINNERS**

SOURCE: Sunburst Communications
　　　　　39 Washington Ave.
　　　　　Pleasantville, NY 10570
HARDWARE: Disks or tapes for Apple II, Commodore PET, or TRS-80
COST: Fifteen titles at $25 each
GRADE RANGE: 3–7
MAJOR SKILLS: Literature appreciation
　　　　　　　Reading comprehension
　　　　　　　Vocabulary

Each of the fifteen titles in this series is based on a different Newberry Award book— one of the most esteemed children's literature honors. The software include vocabulary and comprehension instruction, as well as games. (P)

TITLE: **NURSERY TIME**
SOURCE: Merry Bee Communications
　　　　　815 Crest Drive
　　　　　Omaha, NB 68046
HARDWARE: Disk for Apple II

COST: $30
GRADE RANGE: K–2
MAJOR SKILLS: Print awareness

Two activities are included in this product:

- *Nursery Rhyme* When a child presses one of the keys, the letter is shown on the video screen along with part of an illustrated nursery rhyme. As the rhyme is displayed, the computer plays its associated song.
- *Nursery Story* Illustrations are presented on the screen without text to encourage the child to tell a story about them.

The graphics presentations are very enjoyable, although the pacing is somewhat slow for preschoolers. This program is described on page 48.

TITLE: **OUR WEIRD AND WACKY WORLD**

SOURCE: Educational Activities
          P.O. Box 392
          Freeport, NY 11520
HARDWARE: Disks or tapes for Apple II, Commodore Pet, or TRS-80
          (Atari to be available soon)
COST: $40 each
GRADE RANGE: High school remedial readers
MAJOR SKILLS: Literal comprehension
              Critical comprehension

Each disk presents eight different stories of unusual real events. After reading a story, the student completes eight activities consisting mainly of multiple-choice questions, cloze passages, and sentence scrambles. Students who answer correctly get a cartoon reinforcer, while others get a second try before the correct response is displayed. Additional game-like reinforcers are provided after several successive correct responses. Most questions can be answered correctly without reading the passages and the reinforcers could be perceived as childish by teenagers.

TITLE: **PEAR TREE**

SOURCE: Southeastern Educational Software
          3300 Buckeye Road
          Atlanta, GA 30341
HARDWARE: Disk for Apple II
COST: $40
GRADE RANGE: K–4
MAJOR SKILLS: Word identification
              Phonics

This program contains several language arts, mathematics, and reasoning games. The language arts activities are based on the concentration game, in which students gain points by remembering the locations of two matching cards among several. Children play against the computer and try to find words that begin with the same first letter, or that have a particular sound in common. An editor program allows teachers to customize the game contents. (P)

TITLE: **READABILITY**

SOURCE: Micro Power and Light
12820 Hillcrest Rd., Suite 224
Dallas, TX 75230
HARDWARE: Disk for Apple II
COST: $45

This program employs nine readability formulas: Fry, Dale-Chall, Flesch, Flesch-Kincaid, Fog, ARI, Coleman, Powers, and Holmquist. Results are presented both numerically and graphically.

TITLE: **READABILITY ANALYSIS PROGRAM**

SOURCE: Random House
201 E. 50th Street
New York, NY 10022
HARDWARE: Tape or disk for Apple II or TRS-80
COST: $60

This program employs four different readability formulas: Flesch, Dale-Chall, Fog, and Smog. In addition to a summary readability analysis, the program provides a detailed report that includes counts of the number of syllables, words, and characters in the sample. The disk version allows revision of individual words in the sample to adjust the readability of a passage.

REVIEW: *Educational Technology* (April, 1982).

TITLE: **READABILITY LEVEL ANALYSIS**

SOURCE: Bertamax
311 W. McGraw
Seattle, WA 98119
HARDWARE: Tape or disk for Apple II or TRS-80
COST: $40

Four readability formulas (Dale-Chall, Flesch, Fog, and Smog) may be applied to each passage typed into the computer. The program also provides information on the number of words, unique words, syllables, and sentences per sample. (P)

TITLE: **READING FOR DETAIL**

SOURCE: Learning Well
            200 So. Service Rd.
            Roslyn Hts., NY 11577
HARDWARE: Disk for Apple II
COST: $50
GRADE RANGE: 2–5
MAJOR SKILLS: Reading comprehension

Players compete to win a horse race. Landing on special squares requires students to answer detail-oriented questions from a passage. (P)

TITLE: **READING IS FUN**

SOURCE: Tandy/Radio Shack, local dealers
HARDWARE: Tapes for TRS Color Computer
COST: $15 each
GRADE RANGE: 3–6
MAJOR SKILLS: Literature appreciation
                Vocabulary
                Spelling

This series includes four separate titles, each of which contains an abridged classic, an audio tape and a computer tape. Children can read the story independently, or while listening to the audio tape. The computer activities following the story contain vocabulary and spelling questions.

REVIEW: *Courseware Report Card* (December, 1982).

TITLE: **READINGS IN LITERATURE**

SOURCE: George Earl
            1302 So. General McMullen
            San Antonio, TX 78237
HARDWARE: Disk for Apple II
COST: $30
GRADE RANGE: 4–10
MAJOR SKILLS: Story grammar
                Memorization

This program helps students to memorize selections from twenty-seven famous poems, songs, and speeches. The first two lines of text are presented on the screen. Students must enter the next word by typing its first letter. This cycle repeats itself through the length of the saying. Graphic aids help reinforce student guesses.

TITLE: **RHYMES AND RIDDLES**

SOURCE: Spinnaker Software
215 First Street
Cambridge, MA 02142
HARDWARE: Disk for Apple II
COST: $30
GRADE RANGE: K–3
MAJOR SKILLS: Spelling

Children learn to spell and type by associating letters and words to well-known riddles, rhymes, jokes, and sayings. (P)

TITLE: **SENTENCE MAKER**

SOURCE: Reston Publishing
11480 Sunset Hills Rd.
Reston, VA 22090
HARDWARE: Disk for Apple II
COST: (prepublication)
GRADE RANGE: 3–8
MAJOR SKILLS: Sentence structure
Spelling

This program employs a game format for two players. The game presents a popular five-word saying with only the first letter of each word displayed (e.g., "E D H H D"). Students take turns guessing the saying by typing complete sentences. Points are awarded for each word correctly guessed and for guessing the saying ("Every dog has his day."). Students can also challenge the grammar of their opponent's sentence. Lively and appropriate graphics are used throughout the program. An advanced version allows students to compete by composing as many different sayings from the same five letters as they can. This program is described on pages 84–85.

TITLE: **SESAME STREET LETTER AND NUMBER GAMES**
SOURCE: Texas Instruments
Lubbock, TX
HARDWARE: Texas Instruments 99/4A;
also requires speech synthesizer
and bar-code reader
COST: (not indicated)
GRADE RANGE   K–1
MAJOR SKILLS: Letter recognition

This game uses a special "magic wand" bar-code reader. When the student slides the wand across a series of printed stripes similar to those now used on grocery products, the computer produces synthetic speech. This game permits students to match sounds to letters. (P)

TITLE: **SEQUENCE**

SOURCE: Learning Well
              200 So. Service Rd.
              Roslyn Hts., NY 11577
HARDWARE: Disk for Apple II
COST: $50
GRADE RANGE: 2–5
MAJOR SKILLS: Story grammar

Students are presented a passage with its paragraphs in a scrambled sequence and must rearrange them correctly. (P)

TITLE: **SPEEDREAD +**
SOURCE: Optimized System Software
              10379 Lansdale Avenue
              Cupertino, CA 95014
HARDWARE: Disk for Apple II or Atari
COST: $60
GRADE RANGE: 4–12
MAJOR SKILLS: Speed reading

This tachistoscope program presents single words, multiple phrases, and extended paragraphs. Users can add material. (P)

REVIEW: *Creative Computing* (October, 1982).

TITLE: **SPEED READER**

SOURCE: Davidson Associates
              6609 Groveoak Place
              Rancho Palos Verdes, CA 90274
HARDWARE: Disk for Apple II or IBM Personal Computer
COST: $49
GRADE RANGE: 4–12
MAJOR SKILLS: Speed reading

The disk provides several speed-reading lessons including exercises to train peripheral vision, span of perception, left-right eye movement, and rapid prose reading. Rates can be set from 100 to 2,000 words per minute.

TITLE: **SPELLING BEE**

SOURCE: Edu-Ware Services
              P.O. Box 22222
              Agoura, CA 91301
HARDWARE: Disk for Apple II

COST: $40
GRADE RANGE: K–3
MAJOR SKILLS: Spelling
Phonics

This program provides spelling practice at a variety of levels, each emphasizing a different phonic pattern—from simple two-letter words to digraphs and diphthongs. A teacher management level permits individual student assignments. In each lesson students must spell a word that fits a displayed picture. Correct responses are rewarded with a brief song; incorrect answers are reviewed until mastery.

REVIEW: Creative Computing (October, 1982).

TITLE: **SPELLING BUILDER**

SOURCE: Program Design
95 E. Putnam Ave.
Greenwich, CT 06830
HARDWARE: Tape or disk for Apple II, Atari, or TRS-80
COST: $20
GRADE RANGE: 7–adult
MAJOR SKILLS: Spelling

This program reviews nine distinct spelling rules. After a rule is explained, the program drills students with several words containing the spelling pattern. (P)

REVIEW: Courseware Report Card (September, 1982).

TITLE: **SPELLING RULES**

SOURCE: Micro Power and Light
12820 Hillcrest Rd., Suite 224
Dallas, TX 75230
HARDWARE: Disk for Apple II
COST: $30
GRADE RANGE: 5–adult
MAJOR SKILLS: Spelling

Lessons provide drill in six common spelling rules, followed by a mastery quiz that uses a game format. (P)

TITLE: **STORY MACHINE**

SOURCE: Spinnaker Software
215 First Street
Cambridge, MA 02142
HARDWARE: Disk for Apple II, IBM Personal Computer, or Atari

COST: $35
GRADE RANGE: K–3
MAJOR SKILLS: Reading readiness
                   Initial writing skills

Children create short stories involving up to four separate objects and eleven different actions. The program generates a cartoon depicting the meaning of each sentence formed. Only direct sentences with a simple grammar and unambiguous action can be understood by the program, although several sentences can be combined into a longer story. Overall, it provides a very amusing format for introducing simple stories.

REVIEW: *Electronic Learning* (February, 1983).

TITLE: **STORY MAKER**

SOURCE: Andee Rubin
               Bolt Beranek and Newman, Inc.
               50 Moulton Rd.
               Cambridge, MA 02138
HARDWARE: Disk for Apple II
COST: $30
GRADE RANGE: 3–8
MAJOR SKILLS: Story grammar
                   Writing

This program provides a flexible story structure in which children are given an initial introductory segment and must select the next segment from several choices. This structure repeats itself through several segments until a complete story is composed. The story can be printed on paper if desired. Options exist to compose new story elements, or transform the story into a game by setting a final goal to which students must find a path. This program is described on pages 89 and 90.

REVIEW: *Classroom Computer News* (May, 1982).

TITLE: **SUSPECT SENTENCES**

SOURCE: Ginn and Co.
               191 Spring St.
               Lexington, MA 02173
HARDWARE: Disk for Apple II or Atari
COST: (prepublication)
GRADE RANGE: 7–adult
MAJOR SKILLS: Reading comprehension
                   Awareness of literary style
                   Writing

This program employs a game format for two or more participants, although all need not be present simultaneously. One person inserts a fake sentence into a paragraph taken from a professionally written work. Another person then tries to guess which sentence is the fake. The computer scores the accuracy of each guess and prompts the participants to discuss the insertion and its detection. Space is available for up to forty different passages. This program provides a very imaginative example of how computers can be used to develop complex skills such as awareness of literary style. This program is described on pages 89 and 91.

TITLE: **TEACHING TOOLS SPELLING PACKAGE**

SOURCE: Teaching Tools
P.O. Box 50065
Palo Alto, CA 94303
HARDWARE: Disk for Apple II;
also requires cassette recorder
and special interface
COST: $100
GRADE RANGE: 3–12
MAJOR SKILLS: Spelling

The program uses a special cassette recorder interface that automatically starts and stops the tape. Teachers can create spelling lists containing up to twenty-five words each. After entering the words into the computer, the teacher must also record a tape of the words in the same sequence. During a lesson, the student types the word after hearing it pronounced on the tape.

TITLE: **TRICKSTER COYOTE**

SOURCE: Reader's Digest Services
Pleasantville, NY 10570
HARDWARE: Disk for Apple II
COST: $49
GRADE RANGE: 3–8
MAJOR SKILLS: Vocabulary

This product contains two video games to drill vocabulary. The first game, *Trickster Coyote*, presents a chase game in which players use a marker to touch synonyms of words displayed at the top of the screen. While the concept underlying this game is very creative, its pace is slow. The second game, *Trickster Tag*, requires students to remember the locations of ten hidden words and match them to synonyms shown at the top of the screen. Incorrect matches score points for the coyote. The highly stimulating graphics in this game distract from the goal of improving reading vocabulary.

TITLE: **TRIP TO AN UNKNOWN PLANET**

SOURCE: Avanti Associates
9 Marietta Lane
Mercerville, NJ 08619
HARDWARE: Tape or disk for TRS-80

COST: $19
GRADE RANGE: 3–5
MAJOR SKILLS: Reading comprehension

This program adapts the dynamic storybook concept to a science fiction trip to an unknown planet. The story is enjoyable but brief, containing about twenty episodes. Most episodes require a choice between only two options, making this adventure game less challenging than most.

TITLE: **TUTORIAL COMPREHENSION CRITICAL READING**

SOURCE: Random House
     201 E. 50th Street
     New York, NY 10022
HARDWARE: Disks or tapes for Apple II or TRS-80
COST: $255
GRADE RANGE: 1–3
MAJOR SKILLS: Critical reading

Individual programs drill students in main idea, sequencing, details, inference, and recognizing fact or opinion. Lessons center on Detective Marvo who reveals helpful information about each skill.

TITLE: **VOCABULARY BASEBALL**

SOURCE: J & S Software
     140 Reid Avenue
     Port Washington, NY 10050
HARDWARE: Disk for Apple II
COST: $30
GRADE RANGE: 8–12
MAJOR SKILLS: Vocabulary

This program uses a baseball theme to drill vocabulary words. Each correct response advances runners around the bases, while errors are scored as outs. Several spelling and grammatical errors are present in early versions of this drill.

REVIEW: *Courseware Report Card* (September, 1982).
     Creative Computing (April, 1982).

TITLE: **VOCABULARY—DOLCH**
      VOCABULARY—ELEMENTARY
      CREATE VOCABULARY

SOURCE: Hartley Courseware
     Box 431
     Dimondale, MI 48821

HARDWARE: Disks for Apple II;
           also requires Cassette Control Device
           and cassette recorder
COST: $40 each
GRADE RANGE: 1–3
MAJOR SKILLS: Word identification

Each of these three products uses a similar format. The student reads a word displayed on the video screen and, a moment later, the cassette recorder pronounces the word for the student's benefit. The student then indicates whether he or she has read it correctly. Incorrect words are stored for later study. The DOLCH version displays the Dolch sight-word list. The ELEMENTARY version is keyed to the Harcourt-Brace *Bookmark* basal series, while the CREATE VOCABULARY disk permits customized lists. (P)

TITLE: **VOCABULARY SKILLS**
SOURCE: Milton Bradley
         443 Shaker Road
         East Meadow, MA 01028
HARDWARE: Disk for Apple II
COST: $45
GRADE RANGE: 4–8
MAJOR SKILLS: Vocabulary
                  Structural analysis

Using a muscle-building theme, this program drills students in recognizing root words and affixes, and in using context cues. In the structural analysis portions, the meaning of each affix is introduced before the start of the lesson. In the context portions, students learn diverse context strategies such as contrast and embedded definitions. Each lesson is followed by a check test. Students are rewarded for satisfactory performance by being allowed to play a video game. Printed worksheets supplement the program.

REVIEWS: *Educational Technology* (December, 1982).
          Courseware Report Card (September, 1982).
          Electronic Learning (October, 1982).

TITLE: **VOWELS TUTORIAL**

SOURCE: Hartley Courseware
         Box 431
         Dimondale, MI 48821
HARDWARE: Disk for Apple II;
           also requires Cassette Control Device
           and cassette recorder
COST: $120
GRADE RANGE: 1–4
MAJOR SKILLS: Phonics

The Cassette Control Device enables synchronized speech. Most of the activities present a word with its vowel omitted. After listening to the word, the student types the missing letter. Resources are available for augmenting or editing the word lists.

REVIEW: *The Computing Teacher* (January, 1982).

TITLE: **WHOLE BRAIN SPELLING**

SOURCE: Sublogic Communications
713 Edgebrook Drive
Champaign, IL 61820
HARDWARE: Disk for Apple II
COST: $35
GRADE RANGE: All
MAJOR SKILLS: Spelling

Based on the premise that visualization is an important component of spelling skills, this program supplements lessons with ample use of graphics. The main program contains 2,000 words, with additional lists available in medical, scientific, secretarial, fairy tale, and "a child's garden of words" categories. (P)

TITLE: **WORD-A-TACH**

SOURCE: Hartley Courseware
Box 431
Dimondale, MI 48821
HARDWARE: Disk for Apple II; also a cassette tape recorder
COST: $27
GRADE RANGE: 4–12
MAJOR SKILLS: Speed reading

Words are flashed at one of four preset speeds. Students respond by pronouncing each word into a tape recorder for later review by the teacher. Utilities are provided for adding or editing word lists. (P)

TITLE: **WORD BLASTER**

SOURCE: Random House
201 E. 50th Street
New York, NY 10022
HARDWARE: Disk for Apple II, Atari, or TRS-80
COST: $150
GRADE RANGE: 2–6
MAJOR SKILLS: Word identification
Sentence grammar

The disk contains forty-five word identification lessons, based on a video-game format. A sentence is first displayed with one word deleted. Students use a video cannon to shoot down the correct word from among many words that move across the top of the screen.

REVIEW: *Educational Technology* (January, 1983).

TITLE: **WORD FAMILIES**

SOURCE: Hartley Courseware
P.O. Box 431
Dimondale, MI 48821
HARDWARE: Disk for Apple II
COST: $30
GRADE RANGE: 1–3
MAJOR SKILLS: Phonics

This program uses phoneme substitution drill to practice phonics skills. Children are presented a word and four replacement letters (e.g., BAG, S, W, K, R) and must select the letters that produce a meaningful word when substituted for the underlined letter. All errors are recorded on disk for later review. (P)

TITLE: **WORDMATE**

SOURCE: T.H.E.S.I.S.
P.O. Box 147
Garden City, MI 48135
HARDWARE: Disk for Apple II or Atari
COST: $25
GRADE RANGE: 3–6
MAJOR SKILLS: Compound words

This program presents a computerized adaptation of the "old maid" card game. The player tries to match halves of compound words and avoid getting stuck with the last part. Teachers can insert additional compound words. (P)

TITLE: **WORD PREP**

SOURCE: Micro Power and Light
12820 Hillcrest Rd., Suite 224
Dallas, TX 75230
HARDWARE: Disk for Apple II
COST: $25
GRADE RANGE: 3–12
MAJOR SKILLS: Vocabulary

This program provides a framework for teacher-generated vocabulary lessons. An initial vocabulary of 500 words is included in the program.

TITLE: **WORD SCRAMBLE**

SOURCE: T.H.E.S.I.S.
          P.O. Box 147
          Garden City, MI 48135
HARDWARE: Disk for Apple II, or Atari
COST: $25
GRADE RANGE: 1–4
MAJOR SKILLS: Spelling

A robot prints a word on the screen in scrambled order. The student must rearrange the letters to restore the original word. Additional word lists may be added to the program. (P)

REVIEW: *Courseware Report Card* (December, 1982).

TITLE: **WORDSEARCH**

SOURCE: Hartley Courseware
          Box 431
          Dimondale, MI 48821
HARDWARE: Disk for Apple II;
             also requires printer
COST: $27
GRADE RANGE: All
MAJOR SKILLS: Word identification
                Spelling

This program enables teachers to enter a list of words that are automatically converted into a word search puzzle. The words are listed at the bottom of the page and an answer key is available to the teacher. The teacher can control difficulty by specifying whether or not words can overlap, appear backwards, or along diagonals. (P)

REVIEW: *Courseware Report Card* (September, 1982).

TITLE: **WORD SEARCH PUZZLE MAKER**

SOURCE: Computer's Voice
          2370 Ella Drive
          Flint, MI 48504
HARDWARE: Disk for Atari;
             also requires a printer
COST: $35
GRADE RANGE: All
MAJOR SKILLS: Word identification
                Spelling

The program automatically generates word search puzzles from a list of words entered by the teacher. Teachers can adjust difficulty by specifying whether words are to be hidden horizontally, vertically, or diagonally. Completed puzzles are printed on paper.

TITLE: **WORDS FOR THE WISE**

SOURCE: TYC Software
40 Stuyvesant Manor
Geneseo, NY 14454
HARDWARE: Disk or tape for TRS-80
COST: $35
GRADE RANGE: 1–6
MAJOR SKILLS: Spelling

This program features five separate spelling activities: filling in missing letters in a word, word scrambles, letter matching, alphabetizing, and hangman spelling guessing games. The program has a vocabulary of 1,000 words and teachers can create their own word lists. (P)

TITLE: **WORDSKILL FOR THE MICROCOMPUTER**

SOURCE: Science Research Associates
155 No. Wacker Drive
Chicago, IL 60606
HARDWARE: Disks for Apple II
COST: Six levels at $150 per level
GRADE RANGE: 7–adult
MAJOR SKILLS: Vocabulary
Spelling

This program uses four separate game formats to teach synonyms, antonyms, analogies, and definitions. When students make an error, the correct response is explained. (P)

TITLE: **WORD STRUCTURE**

SOURCE: Borg-Warner Educational Systems
600 West University Drive
Arlington Heights, IL 60004
HARDWARE: Disk for Apple II
COST: $300 per two levels
GRADE RANGE: 3–6
MAJOR SKILLS: Spelling
Vocabulary
Structural analysis

The program provides detailed drill in multiple word identification and vocabulary skills. A management system monitors student progress. (P)

TITLE: **WORDWRIGHT**

SOURCE: Britannica Computer-Based Learning
425 No. Michigan Avenue
Chicago, IL 60611

HARDWARE: Disks for Apple II
COST: $299
GRADE RANGE: Junior–senior high school
MAJOR SKILLS: Vocabulary
                  Spelling

This product contains three separate vocabulary development activities:

- *Fragmentation*   A game in which students combine roots and affixes to form derived words.
- *Crossword*   A vocabulary tutorial and game that builds crossword puzzles for students.
- *Wordsearch*   Creates word search puzzles that students can complete on-line.

All three activities provide students with strong meaning cues including definitions and word usage in sentences. *Fragmentation* is described on page 68.

Index to Commercial Reading Programs

Index

The Authors

Leo D. Geoffrion (Ph.D., The Johns Hopkins University) is currently Assistant Director for Academic Computing at Skidmore College. He was formerly Assistant Professor of Reading at the State University of New York at Albany and Assistant Professor of Education at the University of New Hampshire. Dr. Geoffrion is also the Founder and President of the Communication and Learning Group, Inc., an educational consulting firm, and the author of the Reading software, *Computer-Animated Reading Instruction System.*

Olga P. Geoffrion (B.S., University of Montreal) is a consultant on software production for The Communication and Learning Group, Inc., with specific interests in writing and graphic arts.